CAMBRIDGE STUDIES IN MUSIC

GENERAL EDITORS: JOHN STEVENS AND PETER LE HURAY

Mendelssohn's Musical Education
A Study and Edition of
his Exercises in Composition

CAMBRIDGE STUDIES IN MUSIC

GENERAL EDITORS: JOHN STEVENS AND PETER LE HURAY

Mendelssohn's Musical Education

A Study and Edition of his Exercises in Composition

Oxford, Bodleian MS Margaret Deneke Mendelssohn C. 43

R. LARRY TODD
ASSOCIATE PROFESSOR OF MUSIC
DUKE UNIVERSITY

CAMBRIDGE UNIVERSITY PRESS

CAMBRIDGE

LONDON   NEW YORK   NEW ROCHELLE

SYDNEY   MELBOURNE

Published by the Press Syndicate of the University of Cambridge
The Pitt Building, Trumpington Street, Cambridge CB2 1RP
32 East 57th Street, New York, NY 10022, USA
296 Beaconsfield Parade, Middle Park, Melbourne 3206, Australia

First published 1983

Printed in Great Britain at
the University Press, Cambridge

Library of Congress catalogue card number: 82-9690

British Library Cataloguing in Publication Data

Todd, R. Larry
Mendelssohn's musical education. – (Cambridge studies in music)
1. Mendelssohn, Felix
I. Title
780'.92'4 ML410.M5
ISBN 0 521 24655 5

For my parents

'Merkwürdig ist', sagte ich, 'daß sich von allen Talenten das musikalische am frühesten zeigt, sodaß Mozart in seinem fünften, Beethoven in seinem achten, und Hummel in seinem neunten Jahre schon die nächste Umgebung durch Spiel und Kompositionen in Erstaunen setzten.'

'Das musikalische Talent', sagte Goethe, 'kann sich wohl am frühesten zeigen, indem die Musik ganz etwas Angeborenes, Inneres ist, das von außen keiner großen Nahrung und keiner aus dem Leben gezogenen Erfahrung bedarf. Aber freilich eine Erscheinung wie Mozart bleibt immer ein Wunder, das nicht weiter zu erklären ist. Doch wie wollte die Gottheit überall Wunder zu thun Gelegenheit finden, wenn sie es nicht zuweilen in außerordentlichen Individuen versuchte, die wir anstaunen, und nicht begreifen woher sie kommen!'

'It is remarkable', I said, 'that of all talents the musical shows itself at the earliest stage, so that Mozart in his fifth year, Beethoven in his eighth year, and Hummel in his ninth year already were able to astonish their contemporaries with their performance and compositions.'

'Musical talent', said Goethe, 'probably manifests itself the earliest since music is by its nature instinctive and innate, and requires no great external nourishment or experience drawn from life. But surely a phenomenon like Mozart always remains a wonder which we should not attempt to explain further. But how would the divinity find occasion to cause miracles at any time, if it did not attempt to do so in extraordinary individuals, at whom we gaze, not understanding from where they come!'

Goethe, *Gespräche mit Eckermann*, February 14, 1831

Contents

Facsimiles

Plates I and IV appear by permission of The Pierpont Morgan Library, New York; Plates II, III, V and VI by permission of the Bodleian Library, Oxford.

Preface

We might be tempted to agree with Goethe, who advised against efforts to understand the phenomenal development of musical prodigies; rather, like Eckermann, we might do better to remain in awe. Historians have more or less heeded this advice when considering Mendelssohn. A child prodigy, young Felix showed early his intellectual gifts. By the age of ten, he was translating Caesar and Ovid; by eleven, Horace's *Ars poetica*. Some time during 1820 or 1821 he undertook a humorous attempt at an epic poem, *Paphlëis, ein Spott-Heldengedicht*, written for his brother Paul in dactylic hexameters.[1] He filled notebooks with outlines of European history and studied Greek and landscape drawing. If these pre-adolescent achievements did not quite measure up to those of John Stuart Mill, who read Greek at four years, or Thomas Macaulay, who was blessed with a prodigious memory, Mendelssohn's musical accomplishments more than compensated. He appeared in concert as a pianist at the age of nine; by eleven, he was practicing Kreutzer *Etudes* on the violin and beginning to collect his own compositions, among them *Singspiele*, sacred choral works, and various instrumental pieces.

As a youth Mendelssohn studied composition under the guidance of Carl Friedrich Zelter; he mastered his lessons in music theory, it is thought, with the auspicious facility suggested by his first name. Mendelssohn's composition exercises, the subject of the present study, now permit a more detailed examination of his musical development. Preserved in the Margaret Deneke Mendelssohn Collection of the Bodleian Library, Oxford, Mendelssohn's exercise book is the record of a prodigy, to be sure, but also the record of a child laboriously applying himself to the traditional disciplines of music theory. Unfortunately, the volume is an incomplete record. It begins with advanced exercises in figured bass, concluded on fol. 3v with Zelter's comment 'Ende des Generalbaß'. (Undoubtedly the Bodleian workbook was preceded by exercises which have not emerged; perhaps these, too, will yet surface.) Following this first section, Zelter led his pupil systematically through chorale, invertible counterpoint, canon and fugue in a course which lasted little more than a year, roughly from September, 1819, to January, 1821. Mendelssohn's progress during this time was truly remarkable,

---

1. Ed. International Felix Mendelssohn Society (Basle, 1961).

though he occasionally struggled to master the grammatical 'rules' of his craft, his innate abilities notwithstanding. The exercises are filled with thorough corrections entered by the usually watchful Zelter, particularly in the extensive section devoted to the study of chorale. The composer who would later use chorales – both traditional and freely composed – in a variety of works (including the symphony and the piano trio), who would use *Wachet auf* so masterfully to depict St Paul's spiritual awakening, the same composer made a much more modest beginning in these youthful endeavours of 1819 and 1820.

We have in the workbook, too, some of Mendelssohn's earliest attempts at composition, including several pieces for piano, and for violin and piano. Here Mendelssohn was no doubt encouraged by Zelter to imitate (or emulate) the works of Bach, Mozart, and Haydn – tested models from the eighteenth century. There is little in these compositions that presages the remarkable maturity of a masterpiece such as the Octet, Op. 20 (1825), or the *Sinfonia* No. 9 (1823), the latter only two years removed from the workbook. Rather, we find in them the origins of Mendelssohn's lifelong historical perspective. His revival of the St Matthew Passion in 1829, his intensive study of Handel's oratorios, and the series of historical concerts he presented in Leipzig during the 1830s – these are the understandable consequences of a training rooted in the traditions of eighteenth-century Berlin.

Finally, the workbook documents Mendelssohn's characteristic view of composition as a craft subjected to systematic refinement, in contrast to the more romantic view of music as an expression of spontaneous emotions. The many revisions of his mature scores – one thinks of the different versions of the *Hebrides* Overture or *Die erste Walpurgisnacht*, the revisions for *Elijah* or *Die schöne Melusine* – reflect a critical zeal evident in the exercise book. In his dealings with publishers, Mendelssohn figuratively (and sometimes literally) heeded Horace's advice to the creative artist: 'si quid tamen olim scripseris, in Maeci descendat iudicis auris et patris et nostras, nonumque prematur in annum, membranis intus positis'.[2]

It is a pleasure to record my debts to those who assisted in many ways with the preparation of this study. Thanks are due to Mrs Rosemary Dooley and the series editors of Cambridge Studies in Music, who made many valuable suggestions; to Miss Judith Nagley, Mrs Melanie Crain, and Ms Caroline Usher, who read the MS and proposed some improvements; and to Mrs Susan Wilson, who diligently prepared the final copy. In scope and method this study owes much to Alfred Mann's pioneering work on the pedagogical documents and composition exercises of Handel, Mozart, Haydn, Beethoven, and Schubert. I have discussed several aspects of Mendelssohn's workbook with colleagues; for their forbearance I am very grateful. I would like to thank Miss Margaret Crum (Bodleian Library), Dr

---

2. 'But if you write anything in the future, it should be read before Maecius as critic and your father and me, and it should be kept back for nine years on the parchments inside your desk' (*De arte poetica*, 386-9).

Rudolf Elvers (Staatsbibliothek Preußischer Kulturbesitz, Berlin, BRD), Mr J. Rigbie Turner (The Pierpont Morgan Library, New York), and Professor Tilman Seebass (Duke University) for their assistance. Professor Leon Plantinga (Yale University) offered criticisms on some of this material included in my doctoral dissertation. A grant from the Research Council of Duke University and a Mellon Postdoctoral Fellowship provided the sufficient time and incentive necessary for the completion of the study. I owe gratitude to my wife for her constant encouragement and good humour, and a special debt to my parents, Mr and Mrs T. H. Todd, who have watched with ever increasing curiosity the progress of this study.

R. Larry Todd

Durham, N. C.
April, 1982

Abbreviations

Acta	*Acta Musicologica*
AfMw	*Archiv für Musikwissenschaft*
BamZ	*Berliner allgemeine musikalische Zeitung*
BJ	*Bach Jahrbuch*
BzM	*Beiträge zur Musikwissenschaft*
DJdM	*Deutsches Jahrbuch der Musikwissenschaft*
DSB	Deutsche Staatsbibliothek, Berlin, DDR
HJ	*Händel Jahrbuch*
JAMS	*Journal of the American Musicological Society*
JMT	*Journal of Music Theory*
LAWFMB	*Leipziger Ausgabe der Werke Felix Mendelssohn Bartholdys*
MDM	Margaret Deneke Mendelssohn Collection, Bodleian Library, Oxford
Mf	*Die Musikforschung*
MGG	*Die Musik in Geschichte und Gegenwart*
ML	*Music and Letters*
MN	*Mendelssohn Nachlass,* Deutsche Staatsbibliothek, Berlin, DDR
MQ	*The Musical Quarterly*
MS	*Mendelssohn Studien*
19CM	*19th Century Music*
NYPL	New York Public Library
PML	Pierpont Morgan Library, New York
PQ	*Piano Quarterly*
Rm	*La Revue musicale*
SPK	Staatsbibliothek Preußischer Kulturbesitz, Berlin, BRD
ZfMw	*Zeitschrift für Musikwissenschaft*

Introduction

Since Nottebohm's pioneering edition of Beethoven's studies in composition with Haydn, Albrechtsberger, and Salieri,[1] pedagogical and theoretical documents of prominent composers have generated increasing interest in scholarly circles. Attention has centered principally on several significant sources from the eighteenth century. While we know little about Bach's method of instruction, we do have a series of exercises which Handel devised for Princess Anne.[2] Mozart's tutelage of Barbara Ployer and Thomas Attwood is copiously recorded in manuscripts, in the latter case by a substantial volume transmitting a veritable compendium of exercises in figured bass, species counterpoint, and free composition. As for Haydn, three important sources have survived: the master's annotated copy of Fux's *Gradus ad Parnassum* (faithfully transcribed from the lost original by C. F. Pohl); a summary of Fuxian principles prepared by Haydn in 1789; and the young Beethoven's exercises in species counterpoint with corrections in Haydn's hand.[3]

Comparable materials from the nineteenth century are not as plentiful. Two manuscripts of César Franck's contrapuntal exercises, prepared at the Paris Conservatoire for Antoine Reicha and Henri Berton, were described by Julien Tiersot in 1922; Bruckner's harmony and counterpoint methods, designed for his lectures at the University of Vienna in the 1870s and summarizing his own training with Simon Sechter, appeared in 1950.[4] More recently, Schubert's exercises in species counterpoint and fugue for Salieri and Sechter have attracted attention; and Engelbert Humperdinck's student exercises with Josef Rheinberger have appeared in a critical edition.[5] But we know little about Schumann's work with Heinrich Dorn in Leipzig, Berlioz's or Liszt's study with Reicha in Paris, Chopin's lessons with Elsner in Warsaw, or Brahms' student days in Hamburg. The training of these and other composers cannot be investigated thoroughly for want of suitable documentation.

---

1. Nottebohm, *Beethoven's Studien* I.
2. Mann, 'Eine Kompositionslehre von Händel'; Händel, *Aufzeichnungen zur Kompositionslehre.*
3. Lach, *W. A. Mozart als Theoretiker*; Mozart, *Thomas Attwoods Theorie- und Kompositionsstudien*; Mann, 'Haydn as Student and Critic of Fux', 'Haydn's Elementarbuch', and 'Beethoven's Contrapuntal Studies with Haydn'.
4. Tiersot, 'Les oeuvres inédites de César Franck', pp. 101-7; Bruckner, *Vorlesungen.*
5. See Mann, 'Zu Schuberts Studien'; Irmen, ed., *Engelbert Humperdinck.*

1

Fortunately, this is not the case with Mendelssohn. A bound volume in the Margaret Deneke Mendelssohn Collection at the Bodleian Library, Oxford (shelfmark C. 43), preserves a substantial number of his composition exercises with Carl Friedrich Zelter. Comprising some seventy folios, the volume can be dated roughly from September, 1819, to January, 1821; it represents one of the composer's earliest surviving musical autographs. It is arranged in more or less distinct sections organized around thoroughbass, chorale, invertible counterpoint, and canon and fugue in two and three parts. The exercise book also includes several unknown compositions, including solo piano works and duets for violin and piano, which rank among Mendelssohn's earliest compositions. An inventory of the workbook and a transcription of its contents appear in Part II.

Mendelssohn's workbook is a significant new source of information about Zelter, whose composition method is revealed in detail by the arrangement of the manuscript – and by several colorful comments in the elder musician's gruff handwriting scattered throughout the exercises. Zelter's course of instruction, in turn, reflects a conservative theoretical tradition extending back to J. S. Bach. Zelter himself had been trained by Carl Friedrich Christian Fasch and Johann Philipp Kirnberger, two eighteenth-century Berlin musicians who were contemporaries of C. P. E. Bach. Kirnberger and C. P. E. Bach were both taught, of course, by Johann Sebastian. Kirnberger left what he considered to be a summary of the master's teaching in his magnum opus, *Die Kunst des reinen Satzes in der Musik* (1771-1779). A more or less direct pedagogical line, therefore, may be drawn from Bach through C. P. E. Bach, Kirnberger, and Fasch, to Zelter, and thence to Mendelssohn:

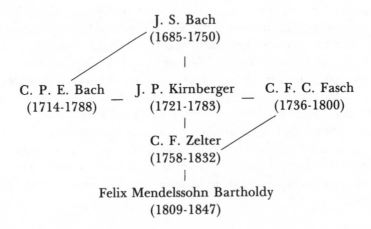

The Deneke MS is thus a new source documenting part of the important theoretical tradition that stems from eighteenth-century Berlin. This tradition played a significant role in Mendelssohn's development – it instilled in him a respect for music of the past; and, if it encouraged in him a decidedly conservative temperament, it provided him with a solid foundation upon which he could build his art.

Mendelssohn's early and rapid rise to musical pre-eminence was by any reckoning astonishing. In September, 1835, at the age of twenty-six, he arrived in Leipzig to assume the directorship of the Gewandhaus Orchestra, an appointment which elicited warm applause from Robert Schumann, who promptly assigned him the honorary sobriquet 'F. Meritis'. Schumann held his distinguished colleague in considerable awe, and with good reason. By the time of the appointment, Mendelssohn enjoyed an international reputation secured by several important works, including his first symphony for full orchestra, the Octet, two string quartets, several romantic concert overtures (*A Midsummer Night's Dream*, *Meeresstille und glückliche Fahrt*, *Die Hebriden*, and *Die schöne Melusine* among them), and two sets of *Lieder ohne Worte* representing a novel type of piano miniature. Schumann, by contrast, had limited his serious composition almost exclusively to piano music; he was still several years away from the productive *Liedjahr* of 1840, and from the fruitful turn to symphonic and chamber works soon thereafter. As the new editor of the *Neue Zeitschrift für Musik* Schumann would have concurred, no doubt, with an earlier estimation of Mendelssohn, voiced by Berlioz in 1831, as one who possessed 'une des capacités musicales les plus hautes de l'époque'.[6] In 1835 Schumann could only publicly marvel at Mendelssohn's creative versatility and privately envy his superior musical education.

This last issue emerged three years later in a letter Schumann wrote to Clara Wieck, in which he attributed Mendelssohn's early musical maturation to his prosperous family circumstances.[7] Though Schumann's remark, perhaps, was prompted by resentment, it had some justification. As the grandson of the noted Enlightenment philosopher Moses Mendelssohn and the son of a well-to-do banker Abraham Mendelssohn Bartholdy, young Felix was exposed to outstanding literary and musical figures of the day. Relatives included on his father's side Dorothea Veit, the wife of Friedrich von Schlegel, co-founder of the Jena school of romanticism; and on his mother's side Sarah Levy, a patroness of C. P. E. Bach and former pupil of Wilhelm Friedemann Bach. His composition teacher, Carl Friedrich Zelter, was the musical adviser and confidant of Goethe. Moreover, Mendelssohn studied piano with several fashionable virtuosi, among them Marie Bigot (an acquaintance of Haydn and Beethoven), Ludwig Berger (a former pupil of Clementi), Hummel, and Moscheles, in addition to following an ambitious schedule of academic disciplines with private tutors. As an adolescent he attended lectures of Hegel, Humboldt, and others at the University of Berlin, newly founded by Frederick William III in 1810.[8] Schumann's student experiences, on

---

6. Berlioz, *Correspondance générale* I, p. 441.
7. Clara Schumann, *Jugendbriefe*, pp. 283-84.
8. Mendelssohn's notes for lectures of the geographer Karl Ritter are preserved at the Bodleian Library, Oxford, in two pamphlets entitled 'Geographie von Europa von Carl Ritter' and dated May-August, 1827. Several earlier, undated notebooks with outlines of English and European history, algebra, and trigonometry are also at Oxford.

the other hand, could not have been more dissimilar. Sent against his will to study law in Leipzig, he was denied the opportunity to pursue composition systematically (Schumann was self-taught, apart from a few lessons in figured bass and rudimentary counterpoint from Heinrich Dorn). One can well appreciate the frustration he expressed to Clara in the letter of 1838.

Traces of Schumann's suspicions have surfaced in more recent times and have conditioned modern evaluations of Mendelssohn's musical background. Often Mendelssohn's mature music is viewed as an overly sentimental expression of Restoration Germany. It is thought that the prosperous circumstances of Mendelssohn's youth prevented his developing the depth or artistic cogency of Beethoven or Schumann. Mendelssohn's astonishing precocity and rapid development have often been credited to his auspicious surroundings. It is not too difficult to discover why. Much of our knowledge about Mendelssohn's childhood and student years in Berlin has been handed down to us by Hensel, Devrient, A. B. Marx, Hiller, Moscheles, Droysen, Klingemann, and Schumann, whose accounts began to accumulate after the composer's death in 1847. Without exception these memorial tributes idolize Mendelssohn, and nowhere does their unabashed adulation appear as fervently as in their discussion of Mendelssohn's youth, which is depicted in glowing tones. Moreover, Mendelssohn's letters are often cited in these accounts in an expurgated form, as if to remove indiscreet suggestions of personal inquietude or artistic indisposition.

Not only are the early eulogies unreliable; the collected edition of Mendelssohn's music is alarmingly incomplete, notably in respect of his early years. The composer once remarked to Schumann that he had published only one fifth of his music;[9] as we know today, the bulk of the unprinted work includes *juvenilia* and student compositions that he passed over or deliberately rejected (among which are several *Singspiele*, and various categories of instrumental and sacred choral music). Clearly the unavailability of the student works has hampered a critical assessment of Mendelssohn's early musical development.[10] Indeed, the few student works which Mendelssohn did release are largely responsible for the misconception that the young composer, nurtured in rich cultural surroundings, emerged, much like Pallas Athena, with intellectual instincts intact, and without a protracted or intense study of composition: these works include the three piano quartets, Opp. 1-3, the Octet and the *Midsummer Night's Dream* overture.

This leads us to another area of misinformation: Mendelssohn's training under Zelter. The image of this teacher-student relationship which has endured is one largely dominated by Mendelssohn's precocity. A prime casualty of this view is Zelter. He is generally accepted as an unbending, though simple-minded, taskmaster - much like the wary *Schulmeister* Kinderschreck in Mendelssohn's *Die*

---

9. Robert Schumann, *Erinnerungen*, p. 73.
10. This gap is slowly narrowing with the appearance of the new Leipzig Mendelssohn edition: the string *sinfonie*, the *Singspiel Die beiden Pädagogen*, the *Te Deum* of 1826, and several early concerti have been issued.

beiden Pädagogen[11] for whom 'wo die Fuchtel nur regiert, da wird alles ausgeführt'. Zelter sometimes emerges as a bystander who observed his student's rapid development without seriously contributing to it or altering its course. According to a less charitable view, Zelter actually exerted a negative influence. Thus we read, somewhat out of context, about his disapproval of Mendelssohn's improvisations before Goethe in 1821; and, according to Devrient, his antipathy bordering on resistance to Mendelssohn's proposed revival of the St Matthew Passion in 1829.[12] Finally, in 1824 Zelter admitted Mendelssohn to the pantheon of Bach, Mozart, and Haydn, as if to suggest that the Meisterschüler at the age of fifteen had already exhausted the teacher's resources. It is a primary aim of this study to re-examine Mendelssohn's musical education in the light of his student workbook and to discuss in more detail the course of his musical development from 1819 to 1821.

BERLIN AND THE BACH TRADITION

Throughout his life Mendelssohn exploited any number of opportunities to champion the music of Bach. During his visit in 1825 to Paris, for example, he somewhat brazenly proselytized for German music, as we learn from the following anecdote recorded for his sister Fanny:

You say I should try and convert the people here, and teach Onslow and Reicha to love Beethoven and Sebastian Bach. That is just what I am endeavouring to do. But remember, my dear child, that these people do not know a single note of 'Fidelio', and believe Bach to be a mere old-fashioned wig stuffed with learning. The other day, at the request of Kalkbrenner, I played the organ preludes in E minor and A minor. My audience pronounced them both 'wonderfully pretty', and one of them remarked that the beginning of the prelude in A minor was very much like a favourite duet in an opera by Monsigny. Anybody might have knocked me down with a feather.[13]

The view of Bach as an old pedant stuffed with too much learning was not due to Parisian ignorance alone, for it exemplified a commonly held opinion, widespread even in Germany. Already in Bach's lifetime a reaction had set in against the learned contrapuntal style, or *hohe Schreibart*, which more and more was interpreted as overwrought and, consequently, ungainly; in its place, the new music of the galant age substituted melodic simplicity and harmonic clarity. Thus, Johann Adolph Scheibe, in his well-known attack on Bach published in 1737, had labeled that composer's music as confused, turgid, and even unnatural.[14] Scheibe particularly found fault with Bach's precise and profuse notation of ornaments which cluttered (or worse, concealed) the essential melodic material.

Such sentiments, of course, were quickly countered by a knowledgeable sup-

11. Adapted from Scribe's delightful comedy of 1817, *Les deux précepteurs, ou Asinus asinum fricat*.
12. Karl Mendelssohn Bartholdy, *Goethe and Mendelssohn*, pp. 11-12; Devrient, *Recollections*, pp. 45-55.
13. Hensel, *The Mendelssohn Family* I, p. 127 (Hensel's faulty text has been corrected by a comparison with the original letter, now in NYPL). The two organ preludes were probably BWV 533 and 543; Mendelssohn himself copied the former on December 9, 1822 (*MN* II).
14. Scheibe, *Critischer Musikus* VI, p. 62.

porter of Bach, L. C. Mizler; but during that time of stylistic change Bach's music for the most part was soon forgotten. Musical erudition was now less valued than musical enlightenment. No less a master than Joseph Haydn, after completing a complex, chromatic passage in the slow movement of his Symphony No. 42 of 1771, rejected it for a simpler solution, noting in the margin of the autograph: 'This was written for ears too learned'. Musical learning was not, evidently, quite socially acceptable – it was to be seen, but not heard.

Mendelssohn's tirade against the Parisian indifference to the music of Bach betrays, in some sense, a provincial attitude that could have been fostered only in a few musical centers. One was Berlin, a bastion of conservatism, where the music of the master was revered and cultivated. Berlin was the home for many years of C. P. E. Bach and W. F. Bach; there, also, Bach's legacy as a teacher was perpetuated and his music preserved. At the Singakademie, an institution founded by Fasch in 1791 and directed after his death in 1800 by Zelter, new impetus was given to the rehearsal and performance of older music, especially Bach's. Due to the zealous efforts of these men, a veritable storehouse of Bach's music in autograph and manuscript sources quickly accumulated. Berlin was also a vibrant center of theoretical study and debate, to some extent more famous for its 'preoccupation with words about music . . . than with music itself'.[15] The acrimonious disputes between Kirnberger and Friedrich Wilhelm Marpurg, both theorists in the thoroughbass tradition (the former reactionary in outlook, the latter favorably disposed toward the new theories of Rameau), impelled the first attempt to synthesize in theoretical language the nature of Bach's teaching.

These two traditions in Berlin – one concerned with the performance of Bach's music, the other the discussion of thorny theoretical issues – greatly affected the quality of musical life in Berlin, and strongly determined the course of Mendelssohn's musical upbringing. It is in these traditions of Berlin, then, that the roots of Mendelssohn's training lay.

In the *Gedanken über die verschiedenen Lehrarten in der Komposition, als Vorbereitung zur Fugenkenntniss*, a short pamphlet published in 1782, Kirnberger praised unconditionally the music of Bach, but noted: 'It is regrettable that this great man never wrote any theoretical work about music, and that his teachings have come to posterity only through his pupils'.[16] Though not entirely accurate (Bach did write down a few rudiments of figured bass), such a comment surely fortified Kirnberger's enviable position as a pupil of Bach and lent considerable authority to his judgments as a music theorist.

One might well inquire, in view of Kirnberger's statement, as to the nature of Bach's theoretical teachings. Some evidence is afforded by C. P. E. Bach, who wrote a letter to Forkel entitled 'In Answer to Questions about Bach'. In the ninth section of this frequently cited document he briefly described Bach's teaching:

In composition he started his pupils right in with what was practical, and omitted all the

---

15. Helm, *Music at the Court of Frederick the Great*, p. 223.
16. Kirnberger, *Gedanken*, p. 4.

dry species of counterpoint that are given in Fux and others. His pupils had to begin their studies by learning pure four-part thorough bass. From this he went to chorales; first he added the basses to them himself, and they had to invent the alto and tenor. Then he taught them to devise the basses themselves. He particularly insisted on the writing out of the thorough bass in parts. In teaching fugues, he began with two-part ones, and so on.[17]

As one might expect, the general outline of this method, with its progression from figured bass to chorale and counterpoint, remained the standard approach to composition in Berlin during the late eighteenth and early nineteenth centuries. It was appropriated by Kirnberger; it represented the essence of Zelter's approach; and consequently it formed the core of Mendelssohn's early training in 1819-1821.

C. P. E. Bach's comments about his father's teaching were incorporated into Forkel's monograph *Über Johann Sebastian Bachs Leben, Kunst, und Kunstwerke*, which, published in 1802, was the first significant biographical study of the master. On several occasions during the previous year Forkel had consulted Zelter, for whom he provided a copy of the new essay. Zelter's *Handexemplar*, now in the Houghton Rare Book Library of Harvard University,[18] is extensively annotated with marginalia in his hand, illuminating Forkel's text. In the chapter entitled 'Bach als Lehrer', for example, Forkel assimilated C. P. E. Bach's comments cited above but added this observation about Bach's chorale instruction, not to Zelter's satisfaction: 'He insisted on correct harmony and on each part having a real melodic line . . . The inner parts of his four-part Hymn-tunes are so smooth and melodious that often they might be taken for the melody.'[19]

In his copy Zelter underlined selected words from this passage and, in his commentary, extended Forkel's conception of the chorale with the question:

And is that something different than counterpoint? Above all Bach is to be esteemed and praised for the contrapuntal element, for Bach's unique genius was expressed in counterpoint.

Und ist das etwas andres als Contrapunct? Ueberhaupt ist Bach nur durch das Contrapunctische zu werthen und zu preisen, denn ganz eigentlich genommen war Bachs Genie im Contrapunctischen.

Forkel did not emphasize what was obvious to Zelter – that an exercise in four-part chorale is a contrapuntal as well as a harmonic exercise. The study of chorale, he maintained, should be regarded as a crucial discipline between thoroughbass and fugue, a transitional stage in Bach's teaching between the homophonic and the strict, contrapuntal styles.

A more systematic attempt to describe Bach's teaching method was undertaken by Kirnberger, who aspired to produce a formal theoretical system illustrative of Bach's teaching. At least, as noted earlier, this was the theorist's announced intention; and his treatise *Die Kunst des reinen Satzes in der Musik* was widely accepted as having attained that goal. Forkel, for one, had this to say: 'Those who would acquaint themselves with Bach's method of teaching composition will find

---

17. Trans. in David and Mendel, eds., *The Bach Reader*, p. 279.
18. Described in Jacobi, 'C. F. Zelters kritische Beleuchtung'.
19. Forkel, *Johann Sebastian Bach*, trans. Terry, pp. 95-6.

it fully set forth in Kirnberger's "Correct Art of Composition".'[20] Fasch and Zelter also respected Kirnberger's contribution. Fasch, in fact, referred the young Zelter to Kirnberger for instruction; years later, in his correspondence with Goethe, Zelter still mentioned Kirnberger with admiration. Zelter's own teaching derived considerable strength from *Die Kunst des reinen Satzes*, and Mendelssohn's workbook establishes clearly that the treatise was still held in high esteem in Berlin several decades after its first appearance in the 1770s.

What were the basic theoretical tenets of Kirnberger, this self-proclaimed interpreter of Bach? They can be best understood, perhaps, through a comparison with those of Rameau, which incited a serious polemic between Marpurg and Kirnberger in Berlin.[21] Both Kirnberger and Marpurg counted themselves among the traditional group of figured-bass theorists; but Rameau's new and radical concepts led to much confusion and disagreement amongst professional teachers. Rameau perceived chords as relatively independent, vertical sonorities having their basis in observable acoustical phenomena. Both Kirnberger and Marpurg were affected by this new, rationalistic approach to music theory. Though Marpurg came to be an avowed apologist for Rameau's thought, Kirnberger managed to reconcile certain features of the Frenchman's work with principles of voice leading favored by traditional practitioners of thoroughbass.

Kirnberger and Rameau proposed similar theoretical maxims but derived strangely different meanings. Common to the views of both theorists was the recognition of the triad and dominant-seventh chord as the basic tonal materials. Other harmonic complexes, such as the chords of the ninth or eleventh, could be produced, according to Rameau, from the dominant seventh by means of subposition or by the arbitrary addition of a third or fifth below the root. For Kirnberger, however, these dissonances were not independent entities but harmonic structures regulated by specific musical contexts. Rameau's theory rested upon a scientific explanation for each chord; for Kirnberger, 'musical rather than acoustical validation was the decisive factor in determining the meaning of a chord'.[22] Kirnberger's system constructed a hierarchy of tonal relationships dividing dissonances into several classes. The 'essential' dissonance, or seventh of the dominant-seventh chord, he termed *wesentlich*. Other dissonances he classified as passing tones and suspensions (grouped under *zufällige Dissonanzen*), or unauthentic sevenths, such as those of the diminished-seventh chords (*unwesentliche Dissonanzen*). These miscellaneous, inessential dissonances were construed to be ancillary to the consonant triad or the 'essential', dissonant dominant-seventh chord: that is, their 'tonal meaning' was inevitably usurped by one of these two sonorities.'

Rameau had introduced as an important new analytic tool the fundamental bass (*basse fondamentale*), by means of which he claimed to discover the under-

20. *Ibid*. p. 99.
21. Summarized in Mekeel, 'The Harmonic Theories of Kirnberger and Marpurg'.
22. Mitchell, 'Chord and Context in 18th-Century Theory', p. 227.

lying roots of successive harmonies. Kirnberger, too, adopted the fundamental bass (*Grundbass*) but subjected it to a series of practical rules more in keeping with his preferred explanations of harmonic events. In his hands, the fundamental bass became a highly efficient device with which one could readily reduce a passage, thereby revealing its primary harmonic components. To demonstrate the analytic utility of the *Grundbass*, Kirnberger tediously produced (with the aid of his pupil Johann Abraham Schulz) the fundamental basses of several works, including one of his own fugues and the Fugue in B minor from the first volume of the *Well-Tempered Clavier*.

Kirnberger's theories, incorporating an admixture of conservative and innovative features, project one of the last imposing statements of the figured-bass tradition. With the exception of treatises by Daniel Gottlob Türk (*Anweisung zum Generalbaßspielen*, 1800) and Augustus Frederic Christopher Kollmann (*A Practical Guide to Thorough-Bass*, 1801), Kirnberger's writings were not as influential internationally as one might expect.[23] They did, however, enjoy a posthumous reputation in Berlin in the late eighteenth and early nineteenth centuries and, in particular, they found a sympathetic reader in Zelter. Even as late as 1819 and 1820, while Gottfried Weber was popularizing the Roman numeral as a novel aid for the identification of chords – an aid which eventually supplanted the fundamental bass – Zelter was still using the Kirnbergerian *Grundbass* in Mendelssohn's exercises. From Kirnberger, Zelter borrowed the theoretical basis for much of Mendelssohn's training in composition.

While Kirnberger was acclaimed more as a theorist than a composer,[24] his associate at the court of Frederick the Great and principal teacher of Zelter, C. F. C. Fasch, was recognized in his day more as a composer. Today, most of Fasch's music remains unknown. Indeed, our knowledge of this neglected figure is greatly indebted to a short biographical pamphlet prepared by Zelter, which, printed in 1801, is still the standard source for information about the musician. According to Zelter, Fasch praised Kirnberger's theoretical work highly: 'Moreover Fasch esteemed Kirnberger very much on account of his great service for the art of composition, the musical fundamental bass, and tuning'.[25] Not surprisingly, Kirnberger exercised a profound influence on Fasch's own teaching, described in some detail in Zelter's autobiography:

At first he allowed me to compose according to my inclination. Then we pursued a systematic method, which I preferred more and more as the work became easier. For a long while I wrote four-part chorales before turning to five-part ones. Next we progressed to counterpoint and canon, which gave me intense joy . . . Eventually we did three-part

23. Though in Vienna Beethoven was aware of them; see Kramer, 'Notes to Beethoven's Education'. Kollmann was active in England where he popularized Kirnberger's theories.

24. Zelter, for one, protested in his copy of Forkel: 'auch seine Compositionen sind keineswegs zu schelten. Wenn sie keine Originale sind, so sind sie fließend, auch munter, und geben einen hübschen Mittelstyl zu erkennen' ('But one should certainly not reproach his compositions. Even if they do not display originality, they are still fluent and vigorous, and they represent a charming middle style').

25. Zelter, *Fasch*, p. 60.

composition . . . From here I turned to the so-called character piece and the French dances, and with that the method *per se* was finished and the fugue begun, which I postponed until I might be more prepared for it.[26]

Although Zelter failed to mention thoroughbass in his list of subjects, there can be little doubt that he was well tutored in it before he proceeded to the study of chorale. The main points of his description resemble on several counts the order of topics in Kirnberger's *Kunst*. The consideration of four-part chorale as the norm, and of five-part and three-part writing as special, deferred cases, is attributable to Kirnberger: a discussion of four-part chorale and then five- and even six-part writing occurs in *Die Kunst*. Kirnberger justified this kind of progression in this manner: 'It is best if one begins with four-part writing, since it is not really possible to set two or three parts completely until one can do it in four parts'.[27] From what the evidence reveals, Fasch's treatment of counterpoint also bears comparison to Kirnberger's. In the second part of *Die Kunst* the theorist began with two-part invertible counterpoint followed by canon. Had he completed a *Dritter Theil*, he would have concluded most likely with fugue as the culmination of theory, as did Fasch. Zelter was to observe a very similar sequence of steps several decades later when he was teaching Mendelssohn.

Unlike Kirnberger, Fasch did not commit his didactic principles to paper. He is remembered today chiefly as a performer and collector of Bach's music. In this regard, his main achievement was the founding of the Berliner Singakademie. Beginning modestly in 1791 as 'eine Art von Chor',[28] the society had rapidly expanded by the end of the century to a formidable force of 148 members. Fasch mainly devoted himself to the revival of the sacred music of the past and especially to that of J. S. Bach, which at that time was still widely unknown. Fasch first considered the most conservative of Bach's sacred works, the motets, and in 1794 thoroughly rehearsed *Komm, Jesu, komm*, *Fürchte dich nicht*, and *Singet dem Herrn ein neues Lied*.[29]

Fasch's successor, Zelter, further explored the riches of Bach's music. For some time he continued to pore over the motets; even when Mendelssohn began his study of thoroughbass in 1819 with Zelter, these works were still being rehearsed and performed. But Zelter also undertook larger-scale projects, including parts of the B minor Mass and St John Passion; the latter, in fact, was rehearsed nearly fifteen years before Mendelssohn's celebrated revival of the St Matthew Passion in 1829.

Fasch had limited the repertoire of the Singakademie exclusively to sacred vocal music; Zelter eventually established in 1807 the Ripienschule, which provided an outlet for performances of older instrumental music. An active member of this organization was Sarah Levy, Mendelssohn's great-aunt. Levy eventually became

---

26. Schottländer, ed., *Carl Friedrich Zelters Darstellungen seines Lebens*, pp. 155-56.
27. Kirnberger, *Die Kunst* I, p. 142.
28. Zelter, *Fasch*, p. 29.
29. Schünemann, 'Die Bachpflege der Berliner Singakademie', pp. 141-2.

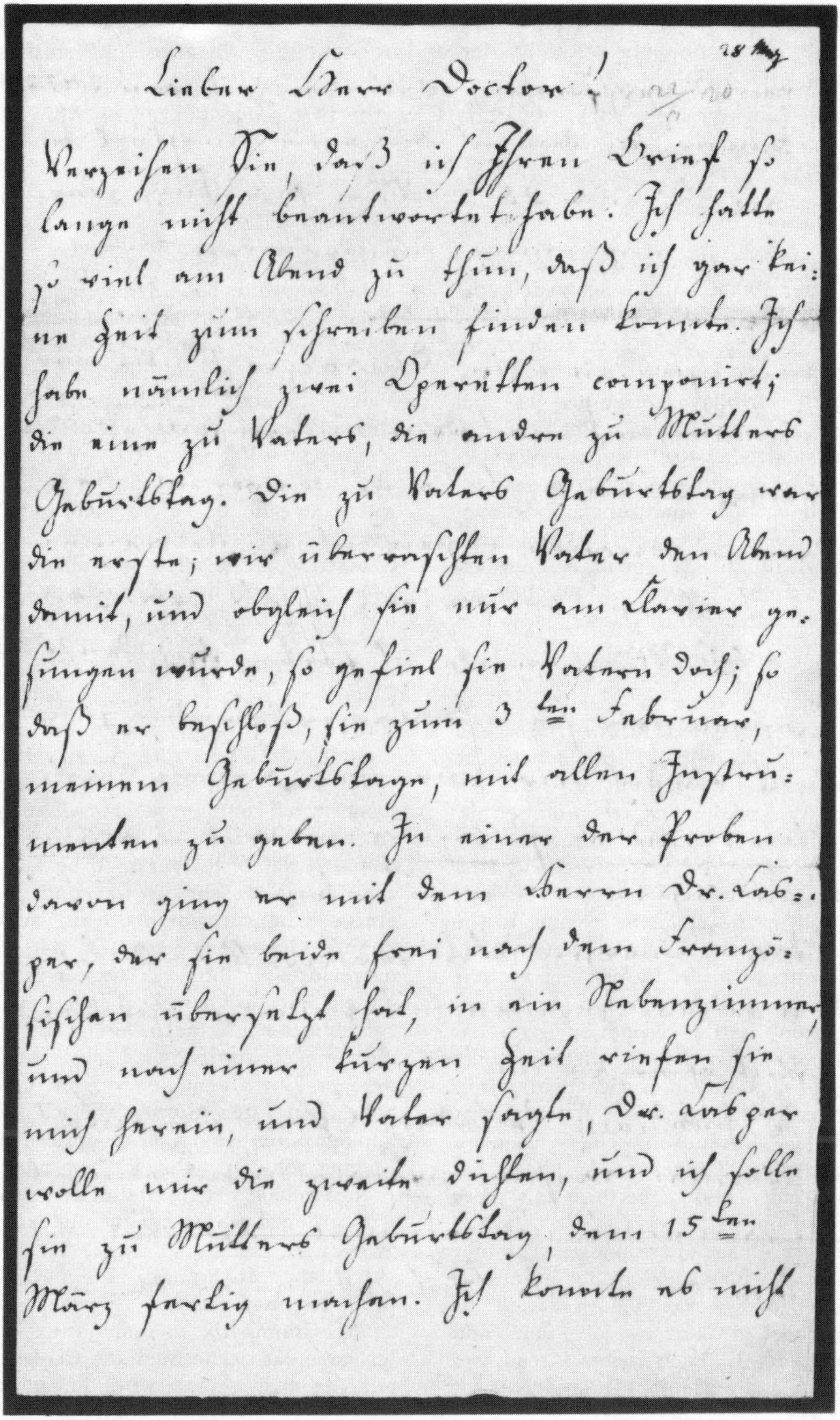

28 May

Lieber Herr Doctor!

Verzeihen Sie, daß ich Ihre Briefe so lange nicht beantwortet habe. Ich hatte zu viel am Abend zu thun, daß ich gar keine Zeit zum schreiben finden konnte. Ich habe nämlich zwei Operetten componiert; die eine zu Vaters, die andern zu Mutters Geburtstag. Die zu Vaters Geburtstag war die erste; wir überraschten Vater den Abend damit, und obgleich sie nur am Clavier gesungen wurde, so gefiel sie Vater doch; so daß er beschloß, sie zum 3ten Februar, meinem Geburtstage, mit allen Instrumenten zu geben. In einer der Proben davon ging er mit dem Herrn Dr. Löbger, der sie beide frei nach dem Französischen übersetzt hat, in ein Nebenzimmer, und nach einer kurzen Zeit riefen sie mich herein, und Vater sagte, der Löbger wolle nur die zweite dichten, und ich solle sie zu Mutters Geburtstag, dem 15ten März fertig machen. Ich konnte ab nicht

Plate I. Autograph letter, dated March 22, 1820

1821. His musical studies, however, constituted only a part of his general education at this time. His equally demanding schedule of academic studies is conveniently summarized for us in a little-known letter (now in the Pierpont Morgan Library, New York: see Plate I for the first page) written on March 22, 1820, to an unidentified doctor:

Dear Doctor,

Please excuse my long delay in answering your letter. I have had so much to do in the evening, that I could not find any time at all to write. I have composed, namely, two operettas – one for Father's, the other for Mother's birthday [December 11 and March 15, respectively]. The one for Father's birthday was the first. We surprised Father with it during the evening, and although it was only sung at the piano, it pleased him so much that he decided to give it with all the instruments on February 3, my birthday.[41] At one of the rehearsals Father accompanied Dr Casper,[42] who had translated both texts freely from the French, into the next room. After a short while they called me in, and Father said that Dr Casper wished to write the second text for me, and that I should have the piece ready for Mother's birthday on March 15. I couldn't exactly promise this, since there was not much time between January 24, when I received the first *Singstück*, and March 15, and I could only devote a few hours in the evening to the project. Nonetheless, I promised to put my best efforts to it. Dr Casper sent me one vocal piece after the other, so I composed them, too. It [the second operetta] has turned out longer than the preceding one, though I spent less time on it. On March 14 I was ready, and on the 15th we sang it at the piano.[43] It went very well, even though we had only three rehearsals, and it has been decided also to perform this piece with instruments . . .

I have six hours of Latin a week: two for Caesar, two for Ovid, one for grammar, and one for exercises. I have started the second book of Caesar, which I don't find difficult at all. Each lesson I read two chapters, and make no translation. As for

Lieber Herr Doctor!

Verzeihen Sie, daß ich Ihren Brief so lange nicht beantwortet habe. Ich hatte so viel am Abend zu thun, daß ich gar keine Zeit zum schreiben finden konnte. Ich habe nämlich zwei Operetten componirt; die eine zu Vaters, die andre zu Mutters Geburtstag. Die zu Vaters Geburtstag war die erste; wir überraschten Vater den Abend damit, und obgleich sie nur am Klavier gesungen wurde, so gefiel sie Vatern doch; so daß er beschloß, sie zum 3ten Februar, meinem Geburtstage, mit allen Instrumenten zu geben.[41] Zu einer der Proben davon ging er mit dem Herrn Dr Casper,[42] der sie beide frei nach dem Französischen übersetzt hat, in ein Nebenzimmer, und nach einer kurzen Zeit riefen sie mich herein, und Vater sagte, Dr Casper wolle mir die zweite dichten, und ich solle sie zu Mutters Geburtstag dem 15ten März fertig machen. Ich konnte es nicht gewiß versprechen, weil die Zeit vom 24sten Januar, an dem ich das erste Singstück bekam, bis zum 15ten März sehr kurz war, und ich nur einige Abendstunden daran wenden konnte. Indessen versprach ich mein möglichstes zu thun. Dr Casper schickte mir ein Singstück nach dem andern, und so componirte ich sie auch. Sie ist länger als die vorige geworden, obgleich ich zu ihr weniger Zeit als zu der vorigen gehabt habe. Den 14ten März wurde ich fertig, und den 15ten sangen wir sie am Klavier.[43] Es ging sehr gut, obgleich wir nur drei Proben gehabt haben, und es ist beschlossen worden, auch sie mit Instrumenten zu geben . . .

Ich habe sechs Stunden Latein wöchentlich, zweimal Caesar, zweimal Ovid, einmal Grammatik, und einmal *Exercitia*. Ich habe das zweite Buch des Caesar, der mir gar nicht schwer wird, angefangen.

Ovid, which is much more difficult for me, I am reading the first book. Each lesson I read and translate about fourteen verses. I am up to the metamorphosis of Daphne.

In mathematics I am reading the fifth book of Euclid, which seems to me to be much more difficult than all the preceding ones.

In addition, with Fanny I have two hours of history, two of arithmetic, one of geography, and one of German language. The violin progresses well – I have two lessons a week and am playing Etudes by Kreutzer. Also on Monday and Tuesday I go to the *Singakademie* where I hear very beautiful things. Professor Zelter is well; he comes to us twice a week . . . My work schedule is so organized, that I always prepare tasks in the evening which I have received in the morning.

Ich lese in jeder Stunde zwei Kapitel, und mache keine Uebersetzung davon. Im Ovid, der mir viel schwerer vorkommt, lese ich das erste Buch, in jeder Stunde ungefähr 14 Verse, und mache eine Uebersetzung davon. Ich bin bei der Verwandlung der Daphne.

In der Mathematik lese ich jetzt das 5te Buch des Euklid, welches mir schwerer als alle andern scheint, welche vorhergehen.

Uebrigens habe ich mit Fanni zusammen zwei Geschichtsstunden, zwei Rechenstunden, einmal Geographie, und einmal Deutsche Sprache. – Mit der Violine geht's so ziemlich, ich habe zweimal in der Woche Stunde und spiele Etuden von Kreutzer. – Auch gehe ich Montag und Dienstag auf die Singakademie, wo ich sehr schöne Sachen höre. Der Herr Professor Zelter befindet sich recht wohl, er kommt wöchentlich zweimal zu uns . . . Mit meinen Arbeitsstunden bin ich jetzt so eingerichtet, daß ich immer den Abend die Arbeiten mache, welche ich den Morgen aufbekomme.

With this letter we have a remarkable glimpse into the pursuits of the industrious eleven-year-old musician. In addition to weekly lessons in theory, violin, Latin (Greek would be added later), Euclidean geometry, arithmetic, geography, and German, and bi-weekly visits to the Singakademie, Mendelssohn still managed to find time to compose. Though we cannot definitely identify the two *Singspiele* written as birthday presents, we can establish their dates at the end of 1819 and beginning of 1820; they must have been written with Zelter's approval and encouragement. At any rate, within the context of this taxing regimen Mendelssohn's composition exercises with Zelter may now be evaluated.

41. The operetta cannot be identified with confidence. A likely candidate, however, is a 'Lied zum Geburtstag meines guten Vaters, den 11ten Dezember', in G major, for voice and piano, in MDM (C. 21, fol. 107). Though Felix did not include the year of the work, his sister Fanny did compose a 'Lied zum Geburtstag des Vaters den 11ten Dezember 1819', now in SPK; see Elvers, 'Weitere Quellen', p. 218. Felix's contribution was for the same date.

42. Johann Ludwig Casper (1796-1864). A close friend of the Mendelssohn family, he provided libretti for several early dramatic efforts by Mendelssohn, including *Die Soldatenliebschaft* (September-November, 1820) and *Die beiden Pädagogen* (January-March, 1821).

43. Again, it is difficult to identify this composition. The first volume of the *Mendelssohn Nachlass* in DSB includes a short dramatic scene evidently from March, 1820 (see Köhler, 'Das Jugendwerk Felix Mendelssohns', p. 20), but with the French text 'Quel bonheur pour mon coeur de toujours aimer, de toujours charmer'; it was first described in Schünemann, 'Mendelssohns Jugendopern', p. 507.

PART I

1 Figured and Fundamental Bass Exercises

Throughout much of the eighteenth century, figured bass survived as an essential part of practical musicianship and as the basis of a musician's training in theory. Thoroughbass manuals, already commonplace in the seventeenth century, multiplied seemingly unchecked in the eighteenth, especially in Germany and Austria. J. S. Bach himself prepared two summaries of thoroughbass principles,[1] which he culled from an earlier manual, the *Musikalische Handleitung* of F. E. Niedt (1700), and perhaps passed on to Kirnberger. C. P. E. Bach allotted considerable space to an exhaustive treatment of the subject in the second part of his *Versuch über die wahre Art, das Clavier zu spielen*, one of the most important treatises of performance practice in the second half of the century. A steady stream of primers was issued during this time by German theorists and musicians such as Kirnberger, Marpurg, Quantz, Daube, Mattheson, Koch, and Sorge, as well as a comparable number published in Vienna and elsewhere.

The proliferation of thoroughbass instruction was largely a response to the continuing demands for continuo playing. By the end of the eighteenth century, however, the discipline had passed its zenith. Evidence of its decline appeared as early as 1779 in an international collection of songs, airs, and operatic arias compiled by Domenico Corri, an Italian musician active in Edinburgh (and eventual father-in-law of Jan Ladislav Dussek). On the title page of his anthology Corri advertised a 'new system' for thoroughbass, which amounted to nothing less than a realization of the figured bass inserted between the treble and bass staves.[2] No doubt this was intended as a crutch for amateurs unskilled in thoroughbass, but it also anticipated the gradual passing of the basso continuo tradition.

There were other signs of decline, even though continuo playing lingered on for years. The elderly Haydn still conducted his London symphonies in the 1790s from the keyboard (harpsichord or fortepiano), much in the same manner as he had done decades before in the service of the Esterházys. As if to reclaim some status for the continuo instrument, the ever-original composer included in the last movement of his Symphony No. 98 (1792) a surprise for the keyboard player: at the very end he allowed the harpsichord to emerge suddenly from the orchestral

---

1. One was intended for Anna Magdalena Bach; the other, as has recently been determined, was copied by Carl August Thieme, perhaps in the 1730s. See Schulze, '"Das Stück in Goldpapier"', pp. 39-41.
2. See Revitt, 'Domenico Corri's "New System"'.

texture to perform a few written-out measures of accompaniment before being engulfed by the boisterous conclusion for full orchestra.

During the early nineteenth century the practical value of figured bass, formerly looked on as its principal raison d'être, was increasingly challenged in theoretical discussions. Gottfried Weber, after expounding some basic thoroughbass principles, strove in several pages of his *Versuch einer geordneten Theorie der Tonsetzkunst* (1817-1821) to defend its usefulness, citing its practical function in the recitative and its application as an analytic method for clarifying complicated passages, or as a shorthand means of quickly recording *in nuce* a sketch for a composition. But, Weber conceded, 'to at least the great majority of readers and players, actual notes would be incomparably more welcome than thorough-base signatures, were it only for the greater clearness with which the music is presented to the eye by notes than by figures'.[3] Other theorists were less forbearing. The Abbé Vogler argued against the inclusion of continuo playing in performances, claiming that it was more or less invalidated by the rapid tempi and complex harmonies of modern music. And Adolf Bernhard Marx, in no sense an adherent of Berlin conservatism, launched a scathing offensive in the first of several 'free' essays entitled 'Briefe über Musik', which appeared in his periodical, the *Berliner allgemeine musikalische Zeitung* in 1827.[4]

Thoroughbass instruction nonetheless persisted for some time in Berlin; during Mendelssohn's student days it even flourished. In 1826 the violinist Ferdinand David corresponded with him about employment prospects in Berlin. He received an encouraging answer from Mendelssohn, who extolled his excellence in figured bass:

There is no question that you can rest assured in this matter, for in addition to your violin playing, you are also excellent and strong in thoroughbass – to my delight, I had an opportunity to convince myself of this. For also, in this branch of music, teachers are sought on all sides. Furthermore, you have the good will and favor of Professor Zelter, who always speaks of you with true devotion, and who has to turn away lessons in thoroughbass on almost a daily basis. His dilemma is to find someone whom he can recommend with good conscience. So – I shall repeat myself – it is at the worst impossible that you will be disappointed.[5]

Some seven years before, Mendelssohn himself had completed a course of exercises in thoroughbass with Zelter, a few of which are preserved in his student workbook and may now be examined.

Only the first three folios of the Oxford MS, in fact, contain figured-bass studies. Clearly, they represent only a portion of the youth's work in the discipline, though no other similar manuscript material has survived. The figures encountered here sometimes involve double and triple suspensions; thus, they suggest a fairly advanced level of thoroughbass, from which we may take for granted

3. Gottfried Weber, *Theory of Musical Composition* II, p. 886.
4. *BamZ* IV (1827), pp. 89-91; see also Thomson, *Voraussetzungen*, pp. 22-27.
5. Felix Mendelssohn Bartholdy, *Briefe aus Leipziger Archiven*, p. 124.

that Mendelssohn had already completed less difficult lessons. Also, these exercises are written entirely in the boy's hand, with no corrections by Zelter. They differ markedly from the contents of the next portion of the manuscript, in which Mendelssohn tried his hand at four-part chorale writing, at first with considerably less success, and with the dutifully critical eye of the teacher. Finally, Zelter's one comment on fol. 3v, 'Ende des Generalbaß Berlin d. 6 October 1819', marks these exercises as the conclusion of Mendelssohn's work in thoroughbass. Presumably, his pupil took up the subject well before October, 1819, perhaps as early as July, when his mother first mentioned Zelter's visits to the Mendelssohn home.

A few initial observations may be made about the organization of the opening folios. For the first eight exercises each page is ruled with nine staves and divided into two systems of four staves each (the ninth staff is left blank). Each exercise involved four stages for Mendelssohn. The first, undoubtedly, was the figuring of the bass, which he presumably worked out with Zelter's supervision and entered on the third staff of each brace (see Plate II). Next, the boy realized the figured bass in a four-part version, recording the soprano, alto, and tenor voices on the second staff of each brace. The order of the third and fourth stages is unclear. On the fourth line of each brace, beneath the figured bass, Mendelssohn notated the fundamental bass, using, as we shall see, Kirnberger's *Grundbass*, and designating each fundamental note with the letter 'd' or 'm' to denote the basic harmony as major ('dur') or minor ('moll'). On the first line of each brace he effected a simplified three-part realization by adding only two new voices above the bass line, instead of the three voices entered on the second staff (he occasionally altered the signatures above the bass line for this reading). Mendelssohn may have completed the three-part setting before determining the fundamental bass. In any event, from the distribution of the staves – the placement of the four-part setting on consecutive staves (the second and third of each brace) and the three-part version on non-consecutive staves (the first and third) – we may surmise that the four-part realization preceded the three-part one. This would be consistent with Kirnberger's insistence on four-part writing as the norm.

Of the nine exercises in the first three folios, seven are transposed versions of the first bass line while the concluding ninth exercise in C major presents a new bass line. Mendelssohn began with C major and progressed through the sharp keys to B major, omitting E major; he then turned to three flat keys, Db, Eb, and F, for the following three exercises. The first eight exercises, despite their common bass lines, are not necessarily transposed copies of each other. Sometimes corresponding sections of the bass line are realized in different ways; furthermore, there are occasional discrepancies in the treatment of the fundamental bass.

Though we have only a bare handful of these exercises, there is much to be learned from them, for they offer specific comparisons with Kirnberger's writings and show concretely how the Bach tradition was transmitted through Zelter's teaching to Mendelssohn. For convenience, the following discussion is organized according to the principal divisions of Kirnberger's theoretical system: the con-

Plate II. Exercise book, fol. 1v

sonant triad, the 'essential' dissonance (or dominant-seventh chord), the 'non-essential' dissonance (including suspensions), and the 'inauthentic' dissonance (or diminished-seventh chord).

In *Die Kunst des reinen Satzes* Kirnberger recognized the major, minor, and diminished triads as consonant tonal structures. The diminished triad, however, he viewed as consonant only in specific contexts. In the major mode, for example, it must act as the dominant of the mediant triad to secure a place as a consonant harmony (ex. la, realized in ex. lb). A diminished triad constructed upon the leading-tone of the tonic was otherwise construed to be an incomplete dominant-seventh chord, and its proper root was located a third below (as illustrated by the fundamental bass added to ex. lc). The opening of Mendelssohn's ninth exercise (fol. 3v) accords with these principles. In the first few progressions there occur two double suspensions, with the signatures $^9_7{}^8_6$. The first resolves to a diminished triad serving as preparation for the second suspension. In agreement with Kirnberger, Mendelssohn interprets the diminished triad as an incomplete dominant-seventh chord and, therefore, considers the G to be the fundamental bass of the complex. The resolution of the subsequent suspension represents the first inversion of the tonic triad, with the fundamental bass a C. Had Mendelssohn chosen B instead of G as the fundamental tone of the first suspension, the result would have been stepwise motion in the fundamental bass (C–B–C), which Kirnberger preferred to avoid in favor of motion by fifths and fourths.[6]

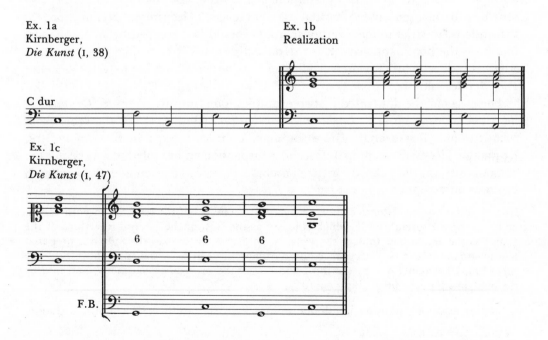

Ex. la
Kirnberger,
Die Kunst (I, 38)

Ex. lb
Realization

C dur

Ex. lc
Kirnberger,
Die Kunst (I, 47)

F.B.

6. Cf. Rameau's usage of the *basse fondamentale* in his analysis of his quintet 'Laboravi clamans' from Psalm 58, given in Rameau, *Treatise on Harmony*; see especially p. 360, m. 3, and p.361, m. 8.

In Kirnberger's view, the diminished triad was not the only sonority with a dualistic interpretation. The highly controversial ${}^6_4$ triad, the *bête noire* of music theorists, was also defined by its context as dissonant or consonant,[7] an approach not as vigorously taken by other theorists. For Kirnberger, there was little question, though, that in its appearance at a cadence as a double suspension, i.e. ${}^{6\,5}_{4\,3}$, the ${}^6_4$ triad invariably drew its meaning from the root of the following ${}^5_3$ triad since the dissonant suspension by definition was not independent or 'essential'. Curiously enough, Mendelssohn's handling of the ${}^6_4$ in this situation varies. The closing progression of the first exercise (fol. 1r) is analyzed in conformity with Kirnberger's principle, yet in other studies the same passage is managed very differently. Thus, in the second and third exercises (fols. 1v-2r) Mendelssohn treats the ${}^6_4$ as consonant and takes the fifth below as its fundamental bass, which yields, in turn, descending stepwise motion in the fundamental bass – at odds with Kirnberger's theory. This contradiction probably owes more to an oversight than a deliberate abandonment of Kirnberger's *Grundbass* in favor of Rameau's *basse fondamentale*, according to which the cadential ${}^6_4$ was viewed as an independent sonority.[8] Oversight might also explain some parallel octaves between the bass and alto near the end of the second exercise (marked by brackets in the transcription) – unnoticed, apparently, by both student and teacher.

Other characteristics of Mendelssohn's fundamental bass rely more strongly on Kirnberger's precedent. The application of the dominant-seventh chord, for example, recalls the theorist's definition of it as the 'essential' or 'authentic' dissonance. Kirnberger had admitted the chord as a legitimate preparation for suspensions. In strict usage, every suspension should be preceded by a consonance; but since the dominant seventh is the only dissonance which (like the consonant triad) is independent, Kirnberger allowed it as an exception to the rule, as Zelter and Mendelssohn were to do.

The case may be illustrated by two examples, one from Kirnberger's *Grundsätze des Generalbasses als erste Linien zur Composition* (Berlin, 1781), the other from Mendelssohn's first exercise. In a summary of rules offered in the *Grundsätze*, Kirnberger licensed the preparation of a suspension in any of three ways: by the consonant triad, the ${}^6_3$ chord, or the consonant ${}^6_4$ chord. He then added the seventh chord as an exception:

Non-essential dissonant tones can be prepared by members of the essential seventh chord, and even by the seventh itself, which is found as the fifth of the ${}^6_5$ chord, the third of the ${}^6_4_3$, and as the actual bass tone of the ${}^4_2$ chord. In Fig. XIII [ex. 2a] the fourth is prepared by the seventh above G of the preceding harmony in *a*; in *b* by the fifth above B of the preceding ${}^6_5$ harmony; in *c* by the third above D of the preceding ${}^6_4_3$ harmony; and in *d* by the bass tone F of the preceding ${}^6_2$ chord.[9]

Similar examples abound in Mendelssohn's first exercise (fol. 1r). Thus, a double

7. Kirnberger, *Die Kunst* I, pp. 50-59.
8. E.g., Rameau, p. 364, m. 8, or Mozart, p. 167, m. 7 and p. 169, m. 7. See also Grant, 'The Real Relationship between Kirnberger's and Rameau's Concept of the Fundamental Bass'.
9. Kirnberger, *Grundsätze* III, p. 72.

suspension near the beginning (rather awkwardly enumerated as $^4_9\,^8_3$) is prepared by the essential dominant-seventh chord in root position; a passage near the middle illustrates preparations of the 2-3, 4-3, and 9-8 suspensions by the chord in its third, second, and first inversions, respectively (simplified in ex. 2b).

As was the custom of the day, Kirnberger distinguished between two styles of writing, the high or strict (*strenge Schreibart*) and the light (*leichte Schreibart*). With the second, less rigorous, manner he indulged in certain freedoms not authorized in the strict style. Mendelssohn, too, in his treatment of suspensions, took advantage of certain liberties recognized by Kirnberger. One concerned the alteration of the bass tone of a suspension upon its resolution. Ex. 3a gives a passage from *Die Kunst* in which the resolution of a 9-8 suspension is accompanied by motion in the bass voice from root position to first inversion. An almost identical progression occurs near the beginning of Mendelssohn's first exercise, in

Ex. 2a
Kirnberger, *Grundsätze* (III, Fig. XIII)

Ex. 2b
Workbook, fol. 1r

Ex. 3a   Ex. 3b   Ex. 3c
Kirnberger,
Die Kunst (I, 77)

which the expected resolution of a 9–8 is again redirected by the figures 9–6. One might argue that the leap in the bass from C to E is necessary in order to avoid parallel octaves between the bass and alto (see ex. 3b). On the other hand, Mendelssohn could have solved the passage as in ex. 3c.

With the diminished-seventh chord, or 'inauthentic' dissonance – the final subdivision of Kirnberger's scheme of chord classification – Mendelssohn took his departure by manipulating the chord in a context more liberal than that afforded by the *leichte Schreibart*. Kirnberger had viewed the diminished seventh as 'inauthentic' because, like the diminished triad in some instances, it could be explained as part of a more fundamental sonority, namely, the dominant-ninth chord. As a result, its proper root was actually a third below the bass tone of the chord.[10] Mendelssohn put this theory into practice in his first exercise, where the fundamental bass of each diminished chord is understood to be a third below the bass voice. The same study shows, however, that the boy used the diminished-seventh chord as a preparation for a double suspension, a formulation not acknowledged by Kirnberger. And in the sixth and ninth exercises (fols. 2v, 3v) the chord introduces a triple suspension: $\begin{smallmatrix}7&9&8\\5&6&5\\&4&3\end{smallmatrix}$. Mendelssohn essentially extended Kirnberger's license by adding the diminished seventh to the dominant seventh as another dissonance suitable for the preparation of a suspension. The freer management of the chord in Mendelssohn's hands owes something, too, to its ever-increasing popularity during the nineteenth century, a time when it would become a figure of topical importance (e.g., the 'Samiel' chord of Weber's *Freischütz*, which Mendelssohn heard at the Berlin premiere in 1821).[11]

To summarize, these few exercises are considerably beholden to Kirnberger's precepts. The analysis of each exercise by means of the *Grundbass*, the explanation of the diminished triad and the diminished-seventh chord as incomplete dominant-seventh and -ninth chords, the inclusion of the dominant seventh as a legitimate dissonant preparation for suspensions, and certain liberties in the suspensions themselves – all of this derives from Kirnberger and underscores the traditional stamp of Mendelssohn's work. Zelter would have recourse again to *Die Kunst* in the chorale exercises following the first section of the workbook. In this second area of study, Mendelssohn, indeed, would enter into the special realm of Bach's own teaching.

10. Kirnberger, *Die Kunst* I, pp. 66-67.
11. So commonplace by 1854 that the theorist Carl Friedrich Weitzmann wrote: 'Er ist in neuerer Zeit so häufig von unseren Tonsetzern benutzt worden, dass es eher einer Schrift bedürfte, welche ihn in engere Schranken zurückzuführen suchte, als einer solchen, welche eine noch weitere Verbreitung dieses Lieblinges der heutigen Musik bewirken wollte' (*Der verminderte Septimenakkord*, Berlin, 1854, 'Vorbericht').

2   Der 'plane' Choralgesang

As one might expect, the chorale was of cardinal importance for the musical education of Mendelssohn and Zelter's other students in Berlin.[1] Germany had witnessed a veritable proliferation of new hymnals during the *Aufklärung*: numerous musicians and poets, as if heedful of Immanuel Kant's challenge 'sapere aude', sought to improve upon the traditional authoritative chorales by contributing fresh, enlightening tunes and texts. Even Mendelssohn as late as 1820, as we shall see, was not immune to this temptation. By the early part of the nineteenth century, however, a reaction had set in – arguments were now presented for the reinstatement of the time-honoured chorales. It was against this background that interest came to be focused on the music of J. S. Bach. For Zelter and Mendelssohn, the cornerstone of Bach's art was the chorale. When Mendelssohn was invited in 1844 to edit a selection of Bach's organ works, many years after his student days in Berlin, he chose to compile only compositions based upon chorale melodies. And when the publisher, Coventry & Hollier, in turn mislabeled several of Bach's chorale preludes as fugues, the discomfited editor protested: 'Why is Bach's name always connected with fugues? He has had more to do with psalm-tunes than with fugues.'[2]

Mendelssohn had more than enough reason, of course, to associate Bach with the chorale. The master had used the chorale as a fundamental part of his teaching, as also had such Berlin musicians as C. P. E. Bach, C. F. C. Fasch, Kirnberger, and Zelter. C. P. E. Bach and Kirnberger, moreover, were involved with the first collected edition of Bach's chorale harmonizations which appeared, after considerable delay, in Berlin in 1765 and 1769.[3] The two musicians remained particularly adamant proponents of chorale instruction. C. P. E. Bach stressed the consummate part writing of his father's chorales, which he viewed as a desirable alternative to 'stiff and pedantic counterpoint', no doubt another salvo directed at Fux's system of species counterpoint.[4] Kirnberger, too, emphasized the propaedeutic value to the would-be composer of four-part chorale writing, and he interspersed numerous examples of Bach's chorales throughout *Die Kunst des*

---

1. Including Eduard Devrient, Otto Nicolai, Carl Loewe, and Gustav Wilhelm Teschner.
2. Letter of December 17, 1844; Mendelssohn, *Letters*, p. 337.
3. See Schering, 'Joh. Phil. Kirnberger als Herausgeber Bachscher Choräle'.
4. From the foreword to the Bach chorales; cited in David and Mendel, eds., *The Bach Reader*, p. 271.

reinen Satzes. Once again, the continuity of the Bach tradition in Berlin at the end of the eighteenth and the onset of the nineteenth centuries is made strikingly evident.

Between October, 1819, and the early months of 1820, Mendelssohn completed a total of thirty-three chorale settings, which divide conveniently into three groups (see the Inventory, pp. 95-96). The first group, roughly half the total, consists of unembellished four-part settings arranged primarily in pairs of related major and minor keys. In the second section, Zelter encouraged Mendelssohn to ornament each exercise after completing a correct four-part setting. Zelter added as a subgroup within this section three special exercises with the chorale melody, normally appearing in the soprano, shifted to the alto, tenor, or bass voice. The third section comprises several original chorales that Mendelssohn himself composed to texts chosen from the *Geistliche Oden und Lieder* of C. F. Gellert. This sequence of studies again reflects Kirnberger's influence; for in Part I of *Die Kunst* Kirnberger examined the chorale first in its simple, undecorated style (*der plane Choralgesang*), then with the addition of embellishment (*der verziehrte Gesang*), and finally with a migrating cantus firmus.[5]

Mendelssohn's preliminary goal was to acquire fluency in the four-part unornamented idiom. To this end, Zelter supplied sixteen textless melodies as cantus firmi in the soprano voice. For certain exercises he merely copied, or instructed Mendelssohn to copy, well-known chorales readily available in Lutheran hymnals. These included: 'Ach, was soll ich Sünder machen' (fol. 8v); 'Allein Gott in der Höh' sei Ehr' (fol. 10r); 'Allein zu dir, Herr Jesu Christ' (fol. 10v); 'Alle Menschen müssen sterben' (fol. 11r); and, in the embellished section of the chorales, 'Freu' dich sehr, O meine Seele' (fol. 13r); and 'Nun danket alle Gott' (fol. 13v). It is perhaps more than coincidence that these melodies appear in strictly alphabetical order; Zelter probably selected them from a readily available chorale collection, perhaps C. P. E. Bach's edition of J. S. Bach's chorales (the first four chorales just cited, in fact, appear in consecutive order in this collection). The openings of at least three other chorales – the first, sixth, and eighth (fols. 4r, 6v, 7v) – are strangely reminiscent of the beginnings of 'Freu' dich sehr, O meine Seele', 'Wer nur den lieben Gott läßt walten', and 'Jesu, meine Freude'; but then they diverge. The remaining melodies appear to have been entirely Zelter's own inventions.

From a note entered by the mentor on fol. 9r we discover how Mendelssohn was to accomplish his task: 'When the bass is finished, it must be tested and improved at the fortepiano without noting the corrections.' ('Muß wenn der Baß fertig ist, auf dem Fortep. probiert und verbessert werden ohne daß die Correctur bemerkt wird'.) The boy thus began by composing a figured bass which he then realized at the keyboard before completing and notating the inner parts. (Mendelssohn wrote each exercise in pencil; after implementing Zelter's corrections, he then traced over his work in ink.) This manner of deriving the figured bass, followed by the

5. Kirnberger, *Die Kunst* I, pp. 141-247.

alto and tenor, basically agrees with Bach's own method, to the extent that we are able to reconstruct it.[6]

Zelter sustains, for the most part, a vigilant watch through nearly every page of the chorales (as we shall see, this would lapse somewhat in later portions of the MS). As a child of ten years, Mendelssohn commits most of the customary errors common to the beginner. A good number of Zelter's improvements, therefore, concern the emendation of parallelisms, cross relations, awkward voice crossings, and other instances of non-idiomatic part writing. Beyond this, however, the basic thrust of his instruction seems to be to imitate and transmit to Mendelssohn various stylistic elements of Bach's chorale settings.

A case in point is the tenth chorale, a setting of 'Ach, was soll ich Sünder machen', which Mendelssohn completed on November 10, 1819 (fol. 8v). Several details of the revised exercise resemble J. S. Bach's version (BWV 259) from the collection C. P. E. Bach made. For example, the final choice of cadences agrees closely with corresponding measures of Bach's setting, as in the extract shown in ex. 4. Like Bach, Mendelssohn preferred the $^6_5$ $^5_3$ close (though sometimes with Zelter's urging, as in mm. 3 and 11). Mendelssohn's bass voice, revamped by Zelter to discourage parallel octaves in mm. 3–4, at first moved through a descent in contrary motion to the soprano; Bach's version opens with a similar type of contrary motion between the outer voices. Finally, at the beginning of the third phrase (m. 9), Mendelssohn directed the bass voice to leap a seventh above, perhaps again in imitation of Bach. (The master's $^6_5$ harmony here, though, is admittedly more convincing than Mendelssohn's trenchant diminished triad.)

Ex. 4
J. S. Bach, BWV 259

Mendelssohn's setting of 'Allein zu dir, Herr Jesu Christ' (fol. 10v), another chorale used intact by Zelter, also betrays Bach's influence – such 'influence', that is, as interpreted by Kirnberger. As a melody several centuries old in origin, it raises the question of modal versus tonal setting, an issue, to be sure, better

---

6. See Introduction, n. 17; Bach's compositional process is examined in Marshall, 'How J. S. Bach Composed Four-Part Chorales'.

comprehended by Zelter than by the young Mendelssohn. Zelter most likely corrected this exercise mindful of principles expounded by Kirnberger. Not only did Kirnberger cite the same melody in *Die Kunst* as an example of the aeolian mode,[7] but, in deference to the age-old tradition of modal ethos, he ascribed to the mode the subjective qualities 'pleasant' and 'charming' ('angenehm' and 'lieblich').[8] As he was quick to acknowledge, Kirnberger based his appreciation of the ancient church modes on the music of J. S. Bach, who, he explained, when setting an old chorale melody, respected the demands of modality: 'I can also show that the most sensitive of the newer composers, J. S. Bach, considered the method of setting chorales according to the old church modes to be essential.'[9] Further, the inherent beauty of the modal melodies should not be vitiated by an ill-advised dependence on tonal settings: 'We have various old church melodies which are so full of feeling and expression that they cannot be converted to the new style without a striking depreciation of their value.'[10] To buttress his argument, Kirnberger arranged two settings of the Lutheran hymn 'Ach, Gott vom Himmel sieh' darein', one in the aeolian mode, and the other – suitably doctored to remove any vestige of *Annehmlichkeit* – in G major (ex. 5a). With a rhetorical outburst the self-appointed judge then rendered this animadversion: 'One would have to be devoid of every feeling not to find the first setting of the melody expressive and excellent, and the second, on the other hand, openly dull and offensive.'[11]

Ex. 5a
Die Kunst (II 1, p. 48)

Ex. 5b
Die Kunst (II 1, p. 61)
Aeolische Tonart

7. Kirnberger, *Die Kunst* II 1, pp. 55-56.
8. *Ibid.* p. 51.
9. *Ibid.* p. 49.
10. *Ibid.* p. 47.
11. *Ibid.*

Kirnberger advocated that a chorale with clear modal features be set modally because he considered modality to be a richer ('reichhaltiger') source for modulation. To demonstrate this, he concocted a table of modulations for the various church modes; his schema for the aeolian mode is given in ex. 5b. Harmonic progressions are arranged here in descending order of preference, according to the principle that longer rhythmic values should be reserved for the more important cadences of a mode. Thus, for the aeolian mode, cadences on the A minor and C major triads are allotted breves; cadences on E major, D minor, and F major, semibreves; and G major, the least serviceable of all, a minim.

Zelter's corrections for 'Allein zu dir, Herr Jesu Christ' expose a similar partiality toward modality. Still present in this exercise are the usual elementary mistakes, including parallel octaves between soprano and tenor in the first two measures – neglected by both teacher and pupil. But of more interest are a few passages highlighting Zelter's preference for a modal rather than a tonal interpretation. Thus, in mm. 13-14 and 17-18 he alters two cadences, not only to ameliorate faulty voice leading but also to instill in this otherwise ordinary exercise a modal character by turning to two deceptive cadences in F major. Zelter's effort certainly would have earned Kirnberger's approval. The raised leading tone G♯, emphasized by Zelter's marking 'gis', is led by half-step to an A in parallel motion with the progression E-F a tenth below in the bass. In *Die Kunst* Kirnberger heartily endorsed such applications of the *subsemitonium modi* (see mm. 1-2 of the aeolian setting in ex. 5a).[12] Zelter's corrections once more prove him to be an orthodox musician, well grounded in Kirnberger's teachings.

Examining these exercises, one is impressed by Felix's persistence in overcoming the intricacies of part writing. At times Zelter voiced his own displeasure, showing himself in an uncompromising light as a rather grim disciplinarian with caustic comments, such as 'this was written without any thought' ('war ganz ohne Gedanke verfertigt', fol. 6v), or in an admonitory tone, 'let me remind you not to take the task too lightly' ('wird erinnert die Sache nicht für gar zu leicht zu halten', fol. 7r, Plate III). One can well imagine the youngster taking these strictures to heart. In any case, with the next section of the manuscript he improved his part writing somewhat and, having redeemed himself, proceeded to the art of chorale embellishment.

---

12. *Ibid.* pp. 42-43.

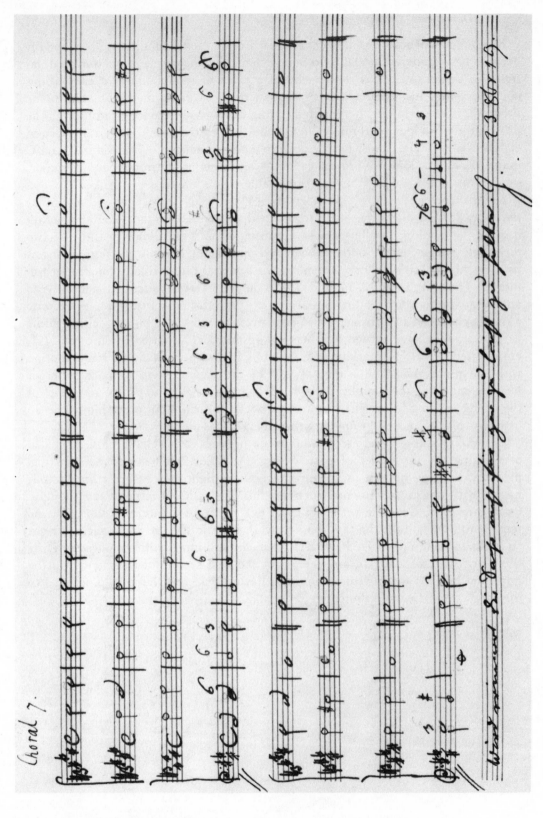

Plate III. Exercise book, fol. 7r

3   Der 'verziehrte' Gesang

Kirnberger described the unornamented, note-against-note character of the chorale as 'plain' or 'even' ('schlecht' or 'gleich'), and further specified this type as *planer Gesang*. Ornamented chorale he labeled *verziehrter Gesang*, or even *verziehrter Contrapunkt*. Just as the unadorned chorale, with its regular succession of rhythmic values, could be compared to ordinary walking, so could the *verziehrter Gesang* be likened to a dance, in which each basic step was executed with a decorative pattern.[1]

Kirnberger asserted that the various ornaments could be conveniently grouped into two principal categories, according to whether or not a given embellishment conflicted with the elementary metrical pulse. As examples of metrically disruptive embellishments, Kirnberger offered the anticipation and suspension (*anticipatio* and *retardatio*). He arranged embellishments compatible with the common pulse into a separate class designated *bunter Contrapunkt*, or mixed counterpoint. In this second division he placed the *Brechung*, or arpeggiation, along with appoggiaturas and an assortment of *durchgehende Töne*, such as passing and auxiliary tones. The *Brechung*, Kirnberger noted, derived directly from an underlying harmony, with pitches of the ornament consonant to the bass. *Durchgehende Töne* comprised a mixture of consonant and dissonant tones. When the dissonance followed an accented consonance, as in an ordinary passing tone, Kirnberger regarded the ornament as a *regulairer Durchgang*; when it preceded the consonance, however, as in an accented passing tone, he classified it as an *irregulairer Durchgang*.

It is this second major division of ornamentation, *bunter Contrapunkt*, which Zelter appropriated for Mendelssohn's work in embellished chorale (fols. 12r-20v). Almost without exception Mendelssohn relied upon two elementary figures representing combinations of the *durchgehende Töne* and the *Brechung*. One is a simple turn-motive in which the principal note of the chorale is decorated by auxiliary and passing tones; the other commences with a leap of a consonant third followed by stepwise contrary motion, thus combining the arpeggiation with a passing tone. Variants of these two are produced by rearranging or inverting the order of each ornament.

Mendelssohn's seventeenth chorale exercise (fol. 12r) illustrates both procedures.

1. Kirnberger, *Die Kunst* I, p. 189.

The first kind of ornament is presented, for example, in m. 2, soprano, and m. 3, bass; its inversion occurs in mm. 5, tenor (canceled) and 6, bass. Instances of the second type appear in m. 1, bass, and m. 5, alto; its derivative is heard in m. 1, tenor, and m. 3, soprano. Just how much these exercises emulate Kirnberger may be judged from an embellished setting of the chorale 'Es ist das Heil uns kommen her' (ex. 6), in which Kirnberger confined himself to the types of ornament just examined in Mendelssohn's study. Admittedly, the theorist's manner of embellishment is more sophisticated, for he frequently added ornaments in two voices simultaneously; and in m. 5 he counterposed two figures related by inversion. But Mendelssohn applied ornaments just as diligently, with one for every minim division, thereby festooning the original *planer Choralgesang* with a flowing quaver motion constantly shifting between the four parts.

From Kirnberger, too, Zelter borrowed the next type of chorale exercise he assigned to Mendelssohn, that with rotating cantus firmi (fols. 14r-15r). Predictably,

Ex. 6
Die Kunst (I, 230)   *Cantus firmus*

we may trace counterparts in *Die Kunst*; similar examples, in fact, are included in Kirnberger's description of embellished chorale.[2] For Kirnberger, it seems, the migrating cantus firmus could be regarded as a contrapuntal elaboration or embellishment of the simple *nota contra notam* chorale style, thus bearing out in another way his term *verziehrter Contrapunkt*.

Of the three possible rotations, moving the pre-existent melody to the bass voice posed, without doubt, the most troublesome exercise for Zelter and Mendelssohn. Kirnberger had already alluded to this: 'The principal voice or *Cantus firmus* can stand in any voice of a polyphonic setting. If you wish to place the *Cantus firmus* in the bass, however, be sure to end with cadences belonging to the key.'[3] And considerably later, in the nineteenth century, A. B. Marx, another Berlin theorist, who for a while was one of Mendelssohn's closest associates, would confront the same problem:

The transposition of the canto fermo into the bass is generally attended with an unpleasant consequence, which may be concealed, but cannot be avoided. Choral [sic] melodies having been originally composed for the upper part, soprano or tenor, the different strains usually terminate with a progression to the second below or above . . . but rarely with a skip to the fourth or fifth. Now as . . . a full perfect close requires the bass to proceed from the dominant to the tonic, it follows that it will almost always be impossible to effect a perfect close, when the canto fermo becomes the bass.[4]

To circumvent this obstacle, Marx devised two remedies, both involving an unavoidable extension of the cantus firmus. The arranger of the chorale could append several measures to obtain either a perfect cadence or a tonic pedal point to bolster the central tonality. In Mendelssohn's exercise (fol. 15r), Zelter resorted to a different stratagem: he simply composed a cantus firmus functioning more as a bass voice than as a chorale melody. He equipped several of the internal cadences in the bass with unmistakable root movement by fifths; and the final cadence required no special alteration, for it formed a perfect cadence by itself. This exercise thus had more to do with the figuring and realizing of a bass than with the transposition of a cantus firmus to the lowest voice.

Neither Kirnberger nor Zelter seems to have placed much emphasis on the migrating cantus-firmus technique. Kirnberger provided several examples but did not discuss the procedure in any detail, while Zelter only included the requisite number of three examples. It is somewhat surprising, perhaps, to find examples elaborated in the writings of Marx, whose treatise cited above did not appear until 1837. Still, the inclusion of the subject in the work of these Berlin musicians is significant, for it portrays them in a conspicuously reactionary stance. Kirnberger's use of the device, not unlike the century-old *vox vagans*, reflects a deliberate withdrawal into the past for didactic models. To a large extent this same conservative attitude persevered well into the nineteenth century – the work of Zelter and the exercises of the young Mendelssohn exude a similar historical spirit.

2. *Ibid*. pp. 161-70.
3. *Ibid*. p. 185.
4. A. B. Marx, *School of Musical Composition*, pp. 315-16.

4   Gellert Chorales

Johann Adam Hiller, a persuasive critic and astute chronicler of eighteenth-century musical taste, was one of the first to urge composers and poets to add to the established repertory of chorales by writing new ones. In his 'Über die Kirchengesänge', which appeared on January 27, 1767, he optimistically proclaimed: 'The exceptional wealth of sacred melodies possessed by our church is indeed to be treasured so highly that one has just cause not only to preserve the melodies, but also to consider augmenting them with new, successful texts and tunes.'[1] Poets such as Gellert, Cramer, and Klopstock wrote new sacred texts, as if to respond to such a call for progress. And many composers, for their part, willingly provided new musical analogues.

The *Geistliche Oden und Lieder* of C. F. Gellert, published in 1757, was one of the most venerated collections, continuing to enjoy the favor of composers well into the nineteenth century. Settings of the poems were of several types. Numerous, nondescript chorale melodies, the most common type, were composed by musicians such as J. F. Doles and Quantz in the eighteenth century, and by J. F. W. Kühnau and M. G. Fischer in the nineteenth – all similar in conception to Hiller's own *Fünf und zwanzig neue Choralmelodien zu Liedern von Gellert* of 1792. Other composers were more innovative, for instance C. P. E. Bach, with his aphoristic Lied settings for solo voice and keyboard, intended for domestic use (Wot. 194); Haydn (a cappella canons, Hob. XXVIIb:7, 8, and 26); Beethoven (song cycle of six Gellert texts, Op. 48); and Carl Loewe (various Lieder).

To these examples we may now add the contribution of the eleven-year-old Mendelssohn who composed, under Zelter's supervision in 1820, chorales for six devotional poems from Gellert's collection as his final exercises in the chorale idiom (fols. 15v-20v, 60v-61r). These pieces are examples of the type popularized by Hiller. Ironically though, Mendelssohn did not aspire to the same ideals espoused by Hiller, who had set forth in a short preface to his chorale collection of 1792 several uncompromising principles of chorale composition:

One teaches them to direct all their energies always to hear the pure consonance of the harmony; one does not permit them to mix in something just for the sake of elegance. There should be no passing tones, no changing tones (if they are not written out, or if it has not been determined that the regular progression of the harmony permits this). One should

1. J. A. Hiller, ed., *Wöchentliche Nachrichten*, I, 237.

allow just as rarely all kinds of flourishes, accents, double appoggiaturas, slides of three and four notes, trills and the like – also a long trill with grace notes on the penultimate note before the cadence. All of these mannerisms are at once beneath the dignity of the chorale, the character of which demands seriousness and the greatest simplicity.[2]

Hiller's directives read as a pointed reaction against Bach's chorales, which were, for the critic's sensibilities, overworked with a complex network of ornate embellishments. Mendelssohn's Gellert studies pose just the opposite – renewed admiration for Bach's chorale style. Accordingly, they are lavishly ornamented, not in the circumspect manner prescribed by Hiller, but after the example of Kirnberger.

In his preface to the *Geistliche Oden und Lieder*, Gellert had recommended that his texts be sung to chorales, viewing them as an indispensable medium through which the proper effect of the poetry was conveyed: 'and just as the declamation of the speaker gives his speech its life, so too the melody gives the text all its strength. Through the musical setting much becomes more impressive and smoother than through reading alone. Many songs must be seen largely from this viewpoint.'[3] To assist his readership, Gellert included an appendix with suggested pairings of poems and well-known chorale melodies. Three of the six texts that Mendelssohn set had been paired by Gellert with popular chorale melodies: 'Gott, deine Güte reicht so weit' to the melody of 'Es ist das Heil uns kommen her'; 'Was ists, daß ich mich quäle' to 'In allen meinen Thaten'; and 'Erinnre dich, mein Geist' to 'Vom Himmel hoch'. Gellert made no suggestions for the other three texts: 'Dein Heil, O Christ, nicht zu verscherzen', 'Was sorgst du ängstlich für dein Leben', and 'Wer bin ich von Natur'. Mendelssohn composed his settings without reference to Gellert's attributions.

'Gott, deine Güte reicht so weit' allows an unusual opportunity to study Mendelssohn's working method. He recorded two versions, on folios 15v and 16r. His first step was the creation of the upper line, in ink; he then proceeded to sketch the remaining parts in pencil. The result was less than satisfactory. Mendelssohn's melody (to the extent we are able to reconstruct it) fits the text awkwardly; the phrase 'so weit die Wolken gehen', for example, is set to an unconvincing descending phrase ending an octave below the opening notes. The part writing moreover is burdened by too many third doublings and by several ungraceful progressions, for example a cadential $^6_4$ triad in the third measure awkwardly ascending to a dissonant seventh chord. Rather than re-work this effort, the boy decided to begin anew by entering a second melody over the original soprano part. He then recopied his new melody on the next page and resumed the task of completing the setting, this time with better results (fol. 16r). Repeating the first two melodic phrases for the third and fourth lines of text, he diverted the harmony to different tonal goals with cadences on the tonic and dominant for the first two phrases answered by cadences on the dominant of the relative minor and on the dominant.

---

2. J. A. Hiller, 'Vorbericht' to *Fünf und zwanzig neue Choralmelodien*, p. xi.
3. Gellert, *Sämmtliche Schriften* II, p. 92.

And to reflect this change, he furnished the parts with a fresh set of ornaments, effectively producing a varied reprise more compatible with Gellert's rhyme scheme of *abab* for the first four lines.

From this unassuming exercise Mendelssohn borrowed substantially for his other Gellert settings. In 'Dein Heil, O Christ, nicht zu verscherzen' (fols. 16v-17r), he availed himself of a triadic figure placed against its counterpart in the bass, as in 'Gott, deine Güte reicht so weit', but here reversed the motives: the soprano begins with an ascending phrase spanning the tonic triad while the bass is fitted with a descending one. For the second phrase, Mendelssohn at first simply re-used that of 'Gott, deine Güte reicht so weit'. He quashed this bit of self-parody, however, by revising a few notes. With the third phrase, though, the lad was guilty of a more serious offense. In its original form the opening resembled the beginning of 'Allein Gott in der Höh' sei Ehr', a chorale he had previously set (fol. 10r). For the fourth phrase, Mendelssohn returned to self-quotation, adopting in this case the second strain of 'Gott, deine Güte reicht so weit'. The tonal organization of this exercise, with its opening phrase structure, V–V–V/VI–V, also ties it to the earlier study.

His next three exercises, settings of Gellert's 'Was ists, daß ich mich quäle', 'Was sorgst du ängstlich für dein Leben', and 'Erinnre dich mein Geist' (fols. 17r-18v), betray similar examples of self-borrowing which need not detain us. With the sixth and final poem, 'Wer bin ich von Natur', the youth produced something more original, though it cost him considerable effort – no fewer than five attempts. In the first two attempts (fol. 19r-19v) he had difficulty establishing a suitable order of cadences. Melodically, the first is marked by a certain staleness and lack of direction. A principal inadequacy is that a tonic is never clearly affirmed. Mendelssohn tried to construe the first setting in G major or modally and the second in G major, as the canceled key signatures indicate. The first ends ambiguously on G, the second on D. The second setting proved acceptable enough to warrant the addition of considerable ornamentation; yet it, too, displays a similar tonal uncertainty. Only with both the third setting (a revision of the first) and the fifth (found considerably later in the manuscript) did Mendelssohn achieve firm final cadences on the tonic (fols. 20r, 60v).

A half-cadence concludes the fourth setting of 'Wer bin ich von Natur' (fol. 20v), but here this ambiguity is justified. In this case Mendelssohn has deliberately devised a melody that is tonally ambiguous. The opening figure, featuring the phrygian configuration E–D–F–E, establishes immediately a modal rather than a tonal context, as does the final peculiar half-cadence on E. The inner cadences waver between the keys of A minor and C major, either stated directly or implied by their dominants:

E	E	A	G	G	E
m. 3	m. 7	m. 12	m. 14	m. 19	m. 25

Mendelssohn's chorale, of course, is not unlike several early chorale tunes that are tonally ambiguous. One of these, 'O Haupt voll Blut und Wunden', had especially aroused the keen interest of Kirnberger, who assembled three harmonizations of it in the phrygian, aeolian, and ionian modes (with his usual objurgatory tone, he opted for the phrygian realization).[4] The mature Mendelssohn would also be attracted to this chorale, well known to him by its frequent appearances in Bach's St Matthew Passion and pre-eminent position at the beginning of Graun's cantata *Der Tod Jesu* of 1755. Like Kirnberger, he would explore its many-sided tonal possibilities.[5]

Mendelssohn's Gellert exercises, along with his other chorale studies, served as sturdy preparation for his subsequent, more mature settings. The prime motivation behind the Gellert chorales, the freedom of the musician to compose original chorales, continued to bear significantly on Mendelssohn's music. We find newly invented chorales, for example, at the conclusion of the Prelude and Fugue in E minor, Op. 35 No. 1, for piano (1837), and in the slow movement of the Cello Sonata, Op. 58, in D major (1843). In a related case, the finale of the Piano Trio, Op. 66, in C minor (1845), the composer took the liberty of altering an existing melody, 'Herr Gott, dich loben alle wir'. These applications are further evidence of the central significance of the chorale which Kirnberger, citing the mastery of Bach's settings, recommended to all composers as 'the best examples for diligent study'.[6]

---

4. Kirnberger, *Die Kunst* I, pp. 221-22.
5. In 1830 Mendelssohn composed a cantata based on this chorale. An edition by the author has appeared in the Yale Collegium Musicum Series (Madison, 1981). See also this author's '*O Haupt voll Blut und Wunden*, a Passion Cantata by Mendelssohn', forthcoming in *American Choral Review*. Mendelssohn's chorale exercise in C major (fol. 31r) appears to borrow the opening of 'O Haupt' for its first phrase.
6. Kirnberger, *Die Kunst* I, p. 157.

5   Invertible Counterpoint

In 1825 Franz Hauser, a young baritone and Bach enthusiast and soon a good friend of Mendelssohn, sought advice for a suitable counterpoint text. He sent an inquiry to Moritz Hauptmann, at that time a court violinist at Kassel but several years later a professor of theory at Mendelssohn's Leipzig Conservatory. Hauser received this reply:

The best way of studying counterpoint? . . . it is hard to be concise and edifying at the same time, if you are to steer clear of platitudes, and if you are not to write a volume on the subject. Kirnberger, though, as far as my memory serves is good (the mobled queen is good, you know); he is more exhaustive, and keeps more to the point than Vogler or Weber, whose pretentious works lose themselves in generalities.[1]

Hauptmann still preferred *Die Kunst des reinen Satzes in der Musik*, even if it was somewhat out of date, to Abbé Vogler's forward-looking *Tonwissenschaft und Tonsetzkunst* (1776) or *System für den Fugenbau* (ca. 1811), or Gottfried Weber's *Versuch einer geordneten Theorie der Tonsetzkunst* (1817-1821), perhaps because of Kirnberger's more practical, matter-of-fact discussion of complex theoretical problems. If Hauser did turn to Kirnberger, he would have found thorough investigations of invertible counterpoint and canon with plentiful examples assembled from the works of G. H. Stözel, Fux, J. S. Bach, C. P. E. Bach, Handel, and Kirnberger himself, as well as others. But he would have missed a discussion of fugue, a discipline not treated in depth by Kirnberger.

To be sure, Zelter in 1820 did not regard Kirnberger as a 'mobled queen' (the First Player's reference in *Hamlet*, II, ii, to the bedraggled, veiled Hecuba fleeing the onslaught of the Greeks in Troy). Nevertheless, he seems to have drawn upon a variety of theoretical sources for Mendelssohn's work in counterpoint, including Kirnberger's *Kunst*, Marpurg's *Abhandlung von der Fuge*, and Fux's *Gradus ad Parnassum*. No doubt, Zelter chose to use such a range of works in order to help fill Kirnberger's lacunae. Nevertheless he chose to follow Kirnberger in the sequence of topics to be studied: exercises in invertible counterpoint; canon in two parts, including the more specialized augmentation and diminution varieties; and finally, at some length, three-part canon, and fugue in two and three parts. This arrangement follows closely the final two subdivisions of *Die Kunst*, entitled 'Von

---

1. A. Schöne and F. Hiller, eds., *The Letters of a Leipzig Cantor* I, p. 1.

dem doppelten Contrapunct' and 'Beschluß von doppelten Contrapuncten', but minus the inclusion of fugal studies.

Zelter designed the first few exercises in invertible counterpoint for Mendelssohn as an effective transition from the preceding chorale settings. He assigned him five separate cantus firmi (fols. 21v-22r), notated in minims with cadences marked by fermatas, giving the appearance of newly composed chorale tunes. (The opening phrase of the first exercise, though, is reminiscent of 'O Welt, ich muß dich lassen'.) The first two cantus firmi are in Zelter's handwriting; the remaining three were recorded – and possibly invented – by Mendelssohn. To the cantus firmi Mendelssohn added a second voice above and below in double counterpoint. The first exercise is fitted with a variety of ornamental tones and suspensions, almost suggesting (were it not for the chorale-like cantus firmus) a study in fifth-species Fuxian counterpoint. The remaining exercises are adorned with an unimpeded flow of quavers, invoking Kirnberger's *verziehrter Contrapunkt*. The spirit of these exercises is expressed by their reliance on the chorale, Kirnberger's 'wahre Grund', which was for Zelter a form with great contrapuntal potential.

A marginal inscription yields some clues as to how the teacher trained Mendelssohn in double counterpoint. At the bottom of fol. 21v Zelter recorded three rules: '1. Not beyond the octave. 2. Not 2 fourths. 3. The ninth to be treated as if it were a second'. Of these, the first is somewhat at odds with Kirnberger and Marpurg. Zelter may have borrowed it, rather, from Fux. The restriction of the octave range between the two voices is explained this way in Fux's *Gradus*:

The limits of the octave are not to be exceeded, because the function of double counterpoint is to produce a different harmonic sound through inversion. If, however, the limits of the octave are exceeded, the same harmonic sound will result, even though the compound consonances are changed to simple consonances, and inversion will result not in different but only in differently placed intervals.[2]

For Fux, then, invertible counterpoint at the octave entailed inversion by only one octave. By this reasoning, a compound interval such as a tenth necessarily 'inverts' to a third, with the result that no true inversion is produced.

To obtain the proper inverted interval (in our example, the sixth), one has to invert, of course, by two octaves instead of the one prescribed by Fux. A provision for this was clearly enunciated by Marpurg in his *Abhandlung von der Fuge*: 'In this type of counterpoint the voices must not range further apart than an octave, if the inversion of the one voice occurs only an octave above or below, while the other voice keeps its position . . . If this limit is surpassed, then the inversion must occur two octaves above or below'.[3] Similarly, Kirnberger, having expanded the definition of inversion to encompass several octaves, denoted specific terms to distinguish the different operations. *Versetzung* corresponds to the procedure, described by Fux, by which a compound interval is merely reduced to its simplest

---

2. Fux, *Gradus*, pp. 176-77; trans. in Mann, *Study of Fugue*, p. 110.
3. Marpurg, *Abhandlung* I, p. 167.

form – without an inversion. *Umkehrung*, on the other hand, produces a legitimate inversion. A third term, *Verwechslung*, describes a strict exchange of parts, by which a given interval is unchanged.[4] Zelter's rather constricting rule limiting Mendelssohn to the octave thus appears indebted to Fux – in point of fact, the octave is not exceeded in any of Mendelssohn's introductory exercises in double counterpoint.

Zelter's second rule prohibits successive fourths, which, when inverted, generate parallel fifths. Without doubt this represents the most fundamental principle of double counterpoint at the octave. It is Kirnberger's and Fux's first rule;, and it may be found in any number of treatises, even as early as Vicentino's *L'antica musica ridotta alla moderna prattica* of 1555.

Zelter's third rule, requiring Mendelssohn to treat the ninth as a second, again points to Kirnberger and Marpurg. Kirnberger approached this issue through the 9–8 suspension (ex. 7a) which, with inversion of one octave, yields the interval of a second followed by a unison, an unacceptable progression for him (ex. 7b). With inversion of two octaves (ex. 7c), the 9–8 suspension is transformed into a 7–8 progression, also undesirable, with the dissonant seventh resolving to an octave. To circumvent this problem, Kirnberger suggested a ready-made solution: as the ninth resolves, the bass moves (ex. 7d), thus removing altogether the 9–8 suspension in double counterpoint.[5] Zelter's directive implies that the ninth should be followed by the tenth (or compound third), so that with inversion of one octave a 2–3 suspension is obtained (exx. 8a, 8b). Inversion of two octaves, in turn, produces an unproblematic 7–6 suspension (ex. 8c). Marpurg substantiated this position: 'In instances where the limit of the octave is surpassed, it should be

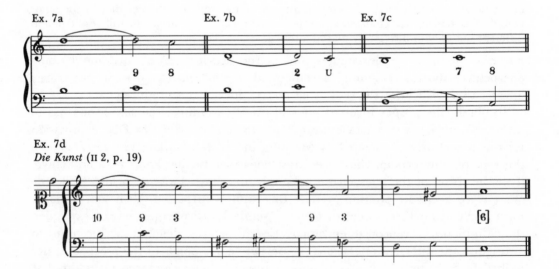

Ex. 7a   Ex. 7b   Ex. 7c

Ex. 7d
Die Kunst (II 2, p. 19)

---

4. Kirnberger, *Die Kunst* II 2, pp. 18-19.
5. *Ibid.*, also I, pp. 77-78.

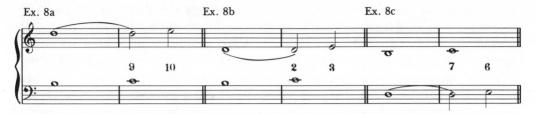

Ex. 8a   Ex. 8b   Ex. 8c

observed that the ninth cannot take its proper resolution in invertible counterpoint. It must be treated not as a ninth, but as a second.'[6] In remarkable contrast, Fux permitted not only the progression 9–8 but also its inversion, 2–1.[7]

There are other principles of the figured-bass school (especially as represented by Kirnberger) which, if not endorsed explicitly by Zelter, were nevertheless observed by Mendelssohn throughout these exercises. Kirnberger described, for instance, particular usages of the fifth in invertible counterpoint. That interval, he said, may not begin or conclude a setting and should be ruled out as well for inner cadences. The reason again concerns the fourth which would make for ungrammatical $^6_4$ chords. The fifth may appear, however, as a diminished fifth, or as a passing tone, either accented or unaccented.[8]

Mendelssohn's exercises essentially conform to these principles. In the first one (fol. 21v) he carefully avoided the fifth on strong beats, allowing it only on weak beats, usually as an ornamental tone (e.g. a passing tone in m. 1, an auxiliary in mm. 5 and 8). He at first wrote a fifth on the downbeat of bar 6 but, noticing his error, canceled it and replaced it with a third. The same measure contains an example of the diminished fifth used as a passing tone, as permitted by Kirnberger. Finally, Mendelssohn circumvented the fifth at the various cadences of his exercise (though not always in other studies; see No. 5, m. 4).

The preliminary studies are followed by three short pieces, all in two parts, in which Mendelssohn tested these procedures in free composition. In the second piece, he actually attempted a strict canon at the octave, with some unpromising results (fol. 22v). Three notes are canceled in the second measure, for example, to avoid parallel octaves two measures later; but despite this precaution, the entry of the second voice ushers in other octaves which remain uncorrected in m. 4. The ungraceful, syncopated figure of m. 6 counteracts the rhythmic continuity of the movement, as does a seemingly uncontrolled series of disjunct leaps just before the cadence on the dominant (mm. 9-13). The other two pieces, in B minor and G major, show a distinct improvement (fols. 22r, 23r-23v). Mendelssohn here evidently took the Bach two-part inventions as his model. In the G major study, the unimpeded motion in quavers, the inversion of the voices in mm. 9-12, and the sequential patterns owe much to Bach.

6. Marpurg, *Abhandlung* I, p. 167.
7. Fux, *Gradus*, pp. 71-73.
8. Kirnberger, *Die Kunst* II 2, pp. 12-17.

The B minor composition is the most successful of the three. Structurally, it represents a typical eighteenth-century form: a binary movement with the tonal plan ‖: i – III :‖‖: III – i :‖ . Thematically, it is decidedly monothematic, another conservative stylistic feature. The turn to the mediant in m. 9 affords Mendelssohn the opportunity to invert the two voices; the material immediately after the double bar is drawn from the original subject, and after the emergence of the tonic in m. 20 the voices are inverted once more (m. 24). Like its predecessors, the B minor study is marked by 'walking' motion in quavers in one voice supported by crotchets in the other. Finally, the treatment of dissonance is regulated by the instructions which Zelter provided for his pupil: ninths or other compound seconds, for instance, are treated as seconds, as in mm. 4–5; and the few fifths which are present fall on weak beats.

There are at least two other autograph copies of the B minor study, one of which permits a relatively precise dating of it. It is found, first of all, in the voluminous archives of the composer's manuscripts at the Deutsche Staatsbibliothek in East Berlin. In the first volume of this collection Mendelssohn placed the study between two movements of an unpublished Piano Trio in C minor, dated April 5–May 9, 1820. If we presume that the youth's exercises in invertible counterpoint were completed around this time, then his progress is truly remarkable. In the space of only a few months, from October, 1819, to early May, 1820, he completed exercises in figured bass, plain and embellished chorale, and invertible counterpoint – certainly an extraordinary feat for an eleven-year-old.

The B minor study was held in some regard by Mendelssohn, for he made another copy of it a few years later. In a manuscript now at the Pierpont Morgan Library it is included with the second piece from the *Sieben Charakterstücke*, Op. 7, and with two other as yet unpublished works.[9] The autograph, inscribed 'für seinen lieben Cousin Arnold', was prepared for Arnold Mendelssohn, probably in March or April, 1826.[10] This version of the piece (Plate IV) includes a tempo indication, 'Allegro molto', and other performance directions lacking in the workbook, as well as revisions (some are included editorially in this edition of the Oxford version). For instance, Mendelssohn improved the closing passages at the end of each section (mm. 13-15, 29-31). In the earlier version of 1820, he had doubled the compound melody of the upper voice an octave below (fol. 22r-22v). Probably dissatisfied by the barren texture (or concerned about the successions of octaves) he reshaped the same measures in the Morgan manuscript by converting the octaves to parallel sixths (ex. 9).

The few exercises in invertible counterpoint contrast sharply in number to the thirty-odd chorale settings set down in the preceding section of the manuscript. Zelter was concerned here only with double counterpoint at the octave, relying

9. The MS is described briefly in Turner, 'Nineteenth-Century Autograph Music Manuscripts', p. 165, and discussed in Todd, 'Instrumental Music', pp. 187-202.

10. Concerning Arnold Mendelssohn see Gilbert, ed., *Bankiers, Künstler und Gelehrte*, p. 313; concerning the dating of the Morgan MS see Todd, 'Instrumental Music', pp. 187-89.

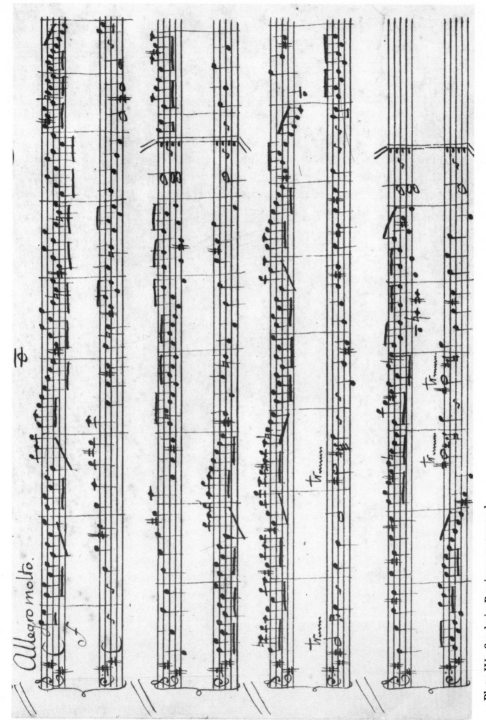

Plate IV. Study in B minor, autograph

Ex. 9
Study in B minor (PML)

entirely upon two-part studies. Beyond this the teacher did not venture. Neither are there three- or four-part assignments, nor an exploration of counterpoint at the tenth or twelfth, standard subjects for Kirnberger and Marpurg. Instead, Zelter now proceeded to a more rigorous discipline, canon.

6   Two-Part Canon

'Canon, among other things, formerly represented the touchstone of harmonic aptitude. Composition in a free style could not be considered sufficient test of one's ability.'[1] With this retrospective comment Friedrich Wilhelm Marpurg introduced his discussion of canon in *Die Abhandlung von der Fuge*. Published in 1753, this treatise, which offered an exhaustive treatment of canonic and fugal technique, was at once an emphatic defense of the music of J. S. Bach and an ambitious attempt to sustain interest in strict contrapuntal forms. It was, moreover, timely. Bach's canonic variations for organ on *Vom Himmel hoch*, *The Musical Offering*, and *The Art of Fugue* – as well as the *Goldberg Variations* (to which we must adjoin the supplementary cycle recently recovered from the master's *Handexemplar*[2]) – were little known at the time, but they provided Marpurg with an unprecedented wealth of contrapuntal refinement and artistry and substantially strengthened his arguments against the evolving aesthetic views of the galant age.

For Bach, canon had been something of an artistic preoccupation. It is not surprising, then, that his closest followers devoted considerable attention to it in their teaching systems. And Mendelssohn's training in canon reflected the continuing strength of the Bach tradition in conservative Berlin. Bach's own preference for canonic writing reflected a longstanding musical tradition; for centuries it had been regarded – as Marpurg recognized – as a primary test of musical prowess. Interest in canon nonetheless declined greatly during the eighteenth century, even when Marpurg was publishing his monumental treatise. Apart from the canonic works of Bach, significant exceptions were canonic cycles such as Telemann's *Sechs Sonaten im Kanon*, Op. V, of 1738, and much later in the century Haydn's cycle of vocal canons, the Ten Commandments (Hob. XXVII a: 1-10). Musicians of the later eighteenth century viewed canon more and more as an abstruse, intellectual curiosity – something in which a composer might occasionally indulge, especially in a minuet[3] – but it was not regarded as a viable art form meriting the extensive efforts that had been expended on it. At the same time, though, canon

1. Marpurg, *Abhandlung* II, p. 51.
2. Discussed in Christoph Wolff, 'Bach's *Handexemplar*'.
3. E.g., Haydn, Symphonies Nos. 42 and 44. For the nineteenth century: Beethoven, Violin Sonata, Op. 96; Schubert, Piano Trio in E♭ major; Dussek, Sonata, Op. 77 (see ex. 10b); and Mendelssohn's Minuet from the first version of the Quintet, Op. 18 (see Todd, 'Instrumental Music', pp. 308-22).

was promoted as a worthy musical skill. Mozart included several examples of it in his lessons with Thomas Attwood, and in the nineteenth century his former rival, Muzio Clementi, incorporated several specimens into his popular piano method, the *Gradus ad Parnassum*. Canon, in short, endured as a traditional academic exercise.

During his twelfth year Mendelssohn wrote several canons for Zelter. Eleven are recorded in a section of the workbook reserved for two-part canon (fols. 23v-30v). Zelter led his pupil through three kinds of exercise. Mendelssohn began with two canons *a 2* at the octave. The next six canons he constructed as examples of invertible counterpoint: in each, the imitating voice was inverted to form a third voice, thus producing two executions for each canon. The final three studies were arranged as a group of canons, two employing augmentation and one diminution.

Mendelssohn composed his first canon upon a subject in F major that Zelter entered in a rough pencil sketch on fol. 22v. In this entry Zelter effected a minor revision in the third measure to avoid a doubled leading-tone on the third beat. Mendelssohn's study, incorporating this improvement, still betrays an unsure hand (fol. 23v). Unable to derive an original continuation of the canon, he simply imitated Zelter's opening motive, characterized by a rising triadic motion through the fifth F–C, and contrived a rather forced cadence in mm. 7 and 8. The result was a division of the exercise into harmonically stagnant two-measure portions with a repetitive unfolding of tenths and sixths.

More serious difficulties, though, emerged in the second canon (fol. 24r), for Mendelssohn here unwittingly wrote a set of parallel octaves in the second half (m. 11). In order to correct the error, Zelter recast the imitating voice a third higher and converted the offensive octaves to tenths. Unfortunately, this minor adjustment caused a further inconvenience, since it required an unwelcomed change in the lower principal voice of the preceding measure (in order to preserve the canon). Had Zelter altered the B♭ and A of m. 10 to D and C♯, parallel octaves would have been obtained in that measure. Unsettled by this turn of events, he canceled his revision in m. 11 and abandoned the unremedied passage.

A problem of a different nature ensues in the following canon (fol. 24r-24v). Labeled 'minore nella 5ta', this is actually the first canon for which Mendelssohn supplied an inverted third voice, in this case at the fourth above. The obstacle here concerns the tonal structure. Like the other exercises, this canon, in C minor, was planned in a simple bipartite form. Ordinarily, one would expect a cadence at the end of the first half in the mediant, E♭ major, or less customarily in the dominant. The tonal scheme of this study is controlled by a sequence of harmonic progressions by fourths, a sequence which leads naturally to the mediant. Mendelssohn, however, continued the exercise one step further. He surpassed the expected mediant and concluded the section on the submediant, A♭ major, in this manner: i-iv-♭vii-III-VI.

In this second group of canons, it would seem, Zelter was more concerned about principles of invertible counterpoint than about elements of tonal organization. To assist his pupil, he provided on the top of fol. 25r the familiar double-row system of numerals for invertible counterpoint at the octave:

$$1 \quad 2 \quad 3 \quad 4 \quad 5 \quad 6 \quad 7 \quad 8$$
$$8 \quad 7 \quad 6 \quad 5 \quad 4 \quad 3 \quad 2 \quad 1$$

To the right of this he also inscribed a series of numerals for double counterpoint at the ninth:

$$1 \quad 2 \quad 3 \quad 4 \quad 5 \quad 6 \quad 7 \quad 8 \quad 9$$
$$9 \quad 8 \quad 7 \quad 6 \quad 5 \quad 4 \quad 3 \quad 2 \quad 1$$

The inclusion of this second diagram is somewhat peculiar, for Mendelssohn's exercises involve counterpoint strictly at the octave; at least, it is strange that Zelter should choose this rare series and not the more standard paradigms for double counterpoint at the tenth or twelfth.

It would be misleading to infer too much from Zelter's marginalia; but it is, perhaps, not insignificant that one theorist in particular treated invertible counterpoint at the ninth in exhaustive detail – Friedrich Marpurg. In his *Abhandlung von der Fuge*, Marpurg actually pondered the relatively minimal discussion of this device in other treatises. Seventeenth-century theorists, such as G. M. Bononcini or Athanasius Kircher, he claimed, had failed to recognize the potential of invertible counterpoint at this interval: Kircher did not mention it at all;[4] while Bononcini rejected it as unwieldy since, in some instances, consonances may invert to dissonances and vice versa (e.g. a second inverts to an octave, a seventh to a third), thus rendering efforts at composition in this species very unpromising.[5] Marpurg, however, quickly dispatched this objection: 'He [Bononcini] must have made a poor study of the subject, since practical experience shows that in counterpoint at the ninth a fifth remains a fifth. It is something different to say that one must observe more restraint in this type of counterpoint than in others. But that does not diminish its worth.'[6] Marpurg then proceeded to bolster his claim by supplying several examples of this neglected type of counterpoint. Perhaps Zelter was aware of Marpurg's interest in inversion at the ninth and for this reason included the appropriate set of numerals, even though he did not require Mendelssohn to complete representative examples.

Many of Mendelssohn's remaining canons are generated from simple melodic sequences conducive to both strict imitation and inversion of the subject. A good example is the fifth canon (fol. 25v), entitled 'Canone alla 2da' and accompanied with an alternative version at the seventh below. This particular study depends upon a series of descending melodic fifths which are readily answered one measure

4. See the discussion of double counterpoint in Kircher, *Musurgia universalis*, pp. 328ff.
5. *Musico prattico*, p. 92.
6. Marpurg, *Abhandlung* I, p. 163.

later at the second above or seventh below, as illustrated by the simple reduction of ex. 10a.

Mendelssohn, of course, was not the only musician to develop canons from melodic sequences. In fact, the progression used in the 'Canone alla 2da' had already been exploited by the pianist-composer Jan Ladislav Dussek. In the minuet of his Sonata, Op. 77 (1812), fancifully dubbed *L'invocation*, Dussek created a 'Canone alla Seconda' modeled on the same sequence of descending fifths (ex. 10b). Dussek's subject is first imitated a seventh below, designated 'Seconda grave'; further on, in the second portion of the movement, he introduced a third voice in parallel thirds, at the same time inverting the answer to a second above, termed 'Seconda acuta'. Dussek, to be sure, masked the basic skeletal design with more compelling craft than did Mendelssohn. Then, too, Dussek interrupted the course of the sequence in m. 5; Mendelssohn's canon, on the other hand, suffers from an excessive reliance on the sequence.

In the following canonic exercises Mendelssohn discovered that the same sequence or a variant could be used to complete canons at other intervals, for instance at the fifth below or fourth above (fols. 25v-26r), and at the third below or sixth above (fols. 26v-27r).[7] For the second exercise, he actually reverted to his original sequence, which at the new interval yields a descending array of sixths, instead of tenths. More importantly, the exercise suggests another comparison

Ex. 10a

Ex. 10b
Dussek, Op. 77

7.   In the latter case, the upper voice should be read an octave higher to obtain the desired inversion. For a similar problem, see the 'Canone alla 5ta' on fol. 26v.

Ex. 10c
Marpurg, *Abhandlung* (I, 8)

with Marpurg, who had proposed the same sequence as an example of *imitatio per arsin et thesin* (ex. 10c).

In his treatise Marpurg ranged comprehensively through the unusual and recondite types of canon, such as the *Krebs* canon, the canon *per tonos*, and the mirror, augmentation, and diminution varieties. Zelter, on the other hand, included only examples of the last two. Two augmentation canons and one diminution canon were completed by his student (again with a third voice added in invertible counterpoint, though not always very successfully; see fols. 28v-30v). Due to the wide ambitus of Mendelssohn's settings, occasionally encompassing three octaves, inversion by even two octaves did not always engender a true inversion (see, for example, m. 4 of the 'Canon in der Verlängerung', fol. 28v). Mendelssohn's exercises in fact alternate freely between genuine double counterpoint and mere transposition of parts, or *Versetzung*, to recall Kirnberger's term.

Mendelssohn's one diminution canon (fols. 28v-29r) posed an intriguing theoretical dilemma, which Marpurg had contemplated in this way:

Diminution canons are actually not possible. Granted, one provides the leading voice with a good 'head start'; but it requires only a moment for the voice in diminution to regain the lead. Where does one then conduct the main voice? From that point, where the beginning voice is matched by the second voice, one has to invert the thing – that is, continue the melody in the second voice and have it answered in augmented values by the first voice. But then we have a mixed canon: at the beginning it belongs to the diminution type, but later on it becomes an augmentation canon.[8]

Marpurg then recommended that the device be confined to fugues, and there only under scrupulous regulation.

Mendelssohn successfully minimized these obstacles by beginning his exercise with an ample eight-measure subject in crotchets. This he then imitated in diminution with four measures of quavers. In turn, the next four measures of the principal voice were compressed into two bars of quavers; and finally, two more measures were reduced to one bar of quavers. A continuation of the canon at this point would have caused the crossing of the voices with an exchange of the *dux* and *comes* roles, so Mendelssohn brought the piece to an abrupt close on the mediant, thus avoiding, *deus ex machina*-like, the pitfalls outlined by Marpurg. To secure an effective approach to the cadence, however, Mendelssohn was compelled to retrace his steps and effect a few minor revisions. For one thing, the

8. Marpurg, *Abhandlung* II, p. 109.

G crotchet of m. 10, appearing first as an unproblematic sixth with the bass, returned in m. 13 as an unwanted dissonance. But more glaring was the leap of a diminished fourth in mm. 12-13 from B♮ to E♭, an unsatisfactory approach to the cadence on E♭ major. These and other passages were altered to insure consistent voice leading and to secure a coherent tonal scheme.

Marpurg, Kirnberger, and Zelter saw canon as a preliminary study for the highest form of counterpoint – fugue. As Marpurg put it: 'One has digressed from the custom [of composing canons]; but the canon will nevertheless always be an indispensable type of composition and will still endure as long as one writes fugues.'[9] The remainder of Mendelssohn's workbook – indeed, over half of the entire document (fols. 31-70) – is filled with fugal exercises.

9. *Ibid.* p. 51.

7   Preliminary Fugal Exercises

In the sixth chapter of Carl Maria von Weber's fragmentary novel, *Tonkünstlers Leben*, there occurs a passage, chiefly concerned with the nature of artistic creation, commenting on the changing status of fugal composition in the early years of the nineteenth century. The protagonist, Felix – not unlike Hoffmann's flamboyant Kreisler – is hard at work on a new composition when he is interrupted by a friend. In the following scene, Diehl marvels at Felix's ability to converse and compose simultaneously:

MYSELF: . . . For I can talk easily and coherently about quite other subjects while I am forming and 'composing' musical ideas with my whole attention . . .

DIEHL: And is this true of all kinds of composition?

MYSELF: No – at least not entirely. With the so-called strict forms, such as fugues and so on, it's harder to combine the two activities.

DIEHL: That's strange, as I should have thought that such things as that needed no great effort of your imagination, only a first-class knowledge of your Kirnberger, your Fux, your Wolf or whatever the brutes are called.

MYSELF: Oh! no, actually it's in abstract work such as this that one has most need of one's feelings to act as guides, so that one doesn't founder in the dry sands of boredom, misled by mere academic fluency.

DIEHL: Then you're not writing any fugues while you're talking so intelligently to me?

MYSELF: You non-musicians really have got your knives into the poor fugues, haven't you? No, I've just composed a song.[1]

Such a dismissal of the fugue as an abstract, mechanical entity mostly devoid of expression was frequently echoed in other accounts by nineteenth-century musicians. Berlioz, recalling in the *Mémoires* his laborious study of counterpoint with Reicha and Lesueur at the Conservatoire, raised a similar complaint: 'I could quote many examples signed by composers who are far greater than Lesueur, but who, in writing them [fugues] merely because it was the convention to do so, have none the less shamefully betrayed their intelligence and committed an unpardonable offence against musical expression.'[2] And Fétis reserved a chapter in his counterpoint treatise (1824) for erudite fugal techniques such as stretto and inver-

---

1. Carl Maria von Weber, *Writings on Music*, p. 357; an excellent discussion of the novel is in Abraham, 'Weber as Novelist and Critic'. Diehl's reference to Wolf is probably to Ernst Wilhelm Wolf (1735-92), a minor composer active in Weimar and the author of *Musikalischer Unterricht* (Dresden, 1788).
2. Berlioz, *Memoirs*, pp. 74-75.

sion, which he entitled, rather sardonically, 'Des artifices par lesquels on évite la monotonie dans la fugue'.[3]

Like canon, however, the study of fugue continued into the nineteenth century as a fundamental discipline, a supreme test of a composer's contrapuntal stamina. Beethoven, of course, had completed several fugues under the guidance of Albrechtsberger; and there is strong evidence that his later experiments benefited considerably from his youthful study.[4] As is well known, Schubert subjected himself shortly before his death to lessons in fugue with that supreme contrapuntist Simon Sechter. Schumann completed several elaborate fugal sketches under the supervision of Heinrich Dorn; he also studied in detail the *Well-Tempered Clavier* and read Marpurg's *Abhandlung von der Fuge*.[5]

Antoine Reicha's *36 Fugues pour piano*, Op. 36 (1803) made a more unusual contribution to the study of fugue. It deserves mention here because it serves as an aesthetic foil to young Mendelssohn's fugal studies. A staunch believer in the inevitability of musical 'progress', Reicha systematically dispensed with traditional techniques of fugal composition. As often as not he answered subjects of his fugues at unpredictable intervals such as the fourth above, the sixth, or even the tritone (the last in a fugue with an equally wayward time signature of 5/4). He considerably augmented the tessitura of the traditional type of subject (e.g. his fugue on the opening of Mozart's *Haffner* Symphony). In several fugues he resorted to asymmetrical, even Bartók-like metrical combinations, all in an effort to improve the fugue, to salvage it from the dry academic sands that Diehl found so objectionable. And yet Reicha also included in his collection an eclectic assortment of fugal subjects extracted from works of Frescobaldi, Domenico Scarlatti, J. S. Bach, Handel, Haydn, and Mozart, as if in deference to the past.

Reicha's Op. 36, which went comparatively unnoticed, was followed by sets of more traditional fugues such as Mendelssohn's keyboard Preludes and Fugues, Opp. 35 and 37, Robert Schumann's cycle of organ fugues on *BACH*, Op. 60, Clara Schumann's *Drei Praeludien und Fugen*, Op. 16, and the more ambitious *Canons et fugues dans tous les tons majeurs et mineurs* of August Alexander Klengel, arranged in two volumes like the *Well-Tempered Clavier*. All of these stand in sharp contrast to Reicha's fantastic experiments. And, not unexpectedly, the young Mendelssohn's work in fugue under Zelter is firmly anchored in eighteenth-century theory and practice. Not reform, but the preservation of a distinguished fugal tradition as epitomized by Bach, is the motivating force behind Zelter's teaching.

We may trace Zelter's method of teaching fugue through several stages. He gave Mendelssohn a few preparatory studies as an introduction to basic fugal method. He then gave him free reign to compose several short fugues in two parts, and

---

3. F.-J. Fétis, *Traité* II, pp. 51-59.
4. See, for example, Kirkendale, 'The "Great Fugue" Op. 133'.
5. Some fugal sketches are reproduced in Roesner, 'Studies in Schumann Manuscripts', pp. 27-49; see also Keil, *Untersuchungen zur Fugentechnik*.

finally required him to compose further canons, and no fewer than eighteen additional fugues, all for three voices. Though these exercises are for the most part undated, a few survive in other autograph copies held in the *Mendelssohn Nachlass* in Berlin (DSB). These concordances (see the Inventory) make it possible to summarize the chronology of Mendelssohn's progress: he began his study of fugue in May, 1820, and finished his three-part exercises in January, 1821, when the workbook was, in all probability, concluded.

A sketch recorded somewhat out of order in the middle of Mendelssohn's two-part canons is the first entry to suggest a fugal texture. At the bottom of fol. 26r Zelter wrote an ascending C major scale in semibreves and fabricated the opening of a countersubject above it in invertible counterpoint. Though the sketch is broken off, Zelter's selection of a scale as a contrapuntal subject is noteworthy in that it typifies his traditional theoretical outlook. Any number of historical precedents might be mentioned. Already in the seventeenth century, the Neapolitan composer Cristofori Caresana had prepared a collection of fugal studies based on *solfeggiamenti*, or scale subjects.[6] The prolific Venetian composer Antonio Caldara included several canons with similar vocalise figures in his *Divertimenti musicali per campagna* of 1729.[7] In 1723 the viol virtuoso Marin Marais published his monumental *La gamme*, a multi-movement trio sonata with its succession of keys arranged in the order of a scale and with conspicuous scale subjects used contrapuntally within movements. And in the 1760s, Haydn composed two fugal movements based on a diatonic scale in his Symphony No. 14 (ex. 11) and in his

Ex. 11
Haydn, Symphony No. 14

Baryton Trio No. 81. (An equally common fugal subject at this time was the chromatic scale which figures in the works of many composers, including such Mannheim musicians as Anton Filz and Xavier Richter.[8])

Zelter's sketch, however, remains an isolated entry; and it is only several folios later in the manuscript that he institutes a systematic treatment of the fugue. On the top of fol. 31v, we read in his handwriting the heading 'Thema, Dux,

6. One appeared in Martini's *Esemplare ossia saggio fondamentale pratico di contrappunto* (1775), and is cited in Mann, *Study of Fugue*, pp. 272-73.
7. Two are in Caldara, *Ein Madrigal und achtzehn Kanons*, ed. Geiringer, p. 14.
8. In F. X. Richter's Adagio and Fugue in G minor, and Anton Filz's *Fuga chromatica*; for others, see Kirkendale, *Fugue and Fugato*, pp. 109ff.

Führer, Soggetto' – Latin, German, and Italian equivalents for the fugal 'subject'. Zelter filled this and the next page with numerous subjects for which Mendelssohn supplied appropriate answers. Zelter's subjects offer a variety of constructions, from straightforward figures in stepwise motion to subjects fashioned with leaps or syncopated figures. Most, but not all, are diatonic; a few contain some chromatic inflections designed, no doubt, to ensnare the pupil. The majority of the subjects do not invoke specific models; one, however (fol. 32r, fifth entry), does appear to have as its prototype the opening of the famous G minor organ fugue of Bach, BWV 578 (ex. 12).

Ex. 12a
Bach, BWV 578

Ex. 12b
Workbook, fol. 32r

Zelter's subjects usually require uncomplicated transposed (or real) answers; only a few need tonal answers. Nevertheless, at times Mendelssohn was unable to differentiate between the two.[9] For Zelter's second entry (fol. 31v) Mendelssohn supplied the correct tonal answer by transforming the original fifth G–C to the fourth C–G. But later on the same page, he was defeated by a subject beginning and ending on the third scale-degree of C major (fol. 31v, fourth entry). In his attempt to derive the answer, he juxtaposed an E with the dominant G (after a less auspicious use of C) and in m. 2 answered the fifth A–D with the unlikely fourth C–G. In the third measure, on the other hand, he suddenly shifted to a real answer and correctly guided the part to the third degree of the dominant, B, a transposition a fourth below the original E.

In his treatise, Marpurg had sought to reduce to a few rudimentary principles the restrictions governing the subject and answer. As he explained, because of the unequal division of the octave into a fifth and fourth, it was possible in certain cases to match either the fourth or fifth scale-degree with the tonic note. This he demonstrated in a table:[10]

c	d	e	f-g	a	b	c	Octave des Haupttons
g	a	b	c	d	e	f-g	Octave der Dominante

He was careful to point out, however, that there were several exceptions to the rule. For example, certain subjects require the fifth and sixth degrees to be

9. For Schubert's difficulties with tonal answers, see Mann, 'Zu Schuberts Studien', pp. 132ff.
10. Marpurg, *Abhandlung* I, p. 31.

answered by the second and third – not by the first and second, as the table indicates. One such case is the Zelter subject just discussed, for which Mendelssohn eventually did discover the correct solution: a straightforward real answer (fol. 31v, fifth entry). Marpurg commented that the 'exception holds whenever the melodic line can be interpreted in terms of the main key or whenever it returns after a brief departure of this kind through a transitional passage to the main key'.[11] The first subject of fol. 32r demonstrates the second possibility. Its first pitch, a B♭, implies a harmonic beginning in the subdominant F major before a definite turn to the tonic C major. In accordance with Marpurg's explanation, the correct answer is a simple transposition pitting the fifth and sixth degrees against the second and third, as Mendelssohn correctly perceived.

11. Mann, *Study of Fugue*, p. 169.

8   Two-Part Fugue

Having acquired some practice with fugal subjects and answers, Mendelssohn went on to write a considerable number of two-part fugues. They are uneven in quality, the product of a youngster struggling to gain experience in fugal composition. Zelter introduced Mendelssohn at this point to the terms *dux* and *comes*, and throughout these exercises Mendelssohn obliged by superimposing the appropriate term for each entrance of the subject and answer, though not always consistently. One further term, *repercussio* or countersubject,[1] appears on fol. 32v, which presents Mendelssohn's first two-part fugue.

Despite these aids, Mendelssohn's early efforts were thwarted by some serious difficulties. As with chorale and canon, he achieved mastery of fugue only after tedious trial and error. His unreliable handling of the subject and answer is most conspicuous in the first exercise. The subject, consisting of a descending fifth followed by ascending stepwise motion, is correctly answered at the outset; but it is subsequently distorted by peculiar metrical displacements and chromatic adjustments. Thus, the *dux* enters one half-measure prematurely in m. 8, countervailing the series of downbeats established in the opening bars. Mendelssohn wrote a metrically correct entrance on the dominant in mm. 14-18, as if to improve the previous passage; but he tampered with the following answer, converting the fifth D–G to the diminished fifth D–G♯ and thus failing to supply the proper tonal answer.

Zelter may well have disapproved, for Mendelssohn reworked the fugue a second time, with better results (fol. 33v). Here he exhibited a surer grasp of the tonal answer and a more persuasive use of chromaticism. For example, he revised a previously confused entrance on D (fol. 32v, mm. 30-34) and thereby made it conform to the diatonic requirements of that scale-degree (fol. 33v, mm. 36-40). He also comprehended more fully the elements of fugal structure. In the second version, he interjected some episodic material to break up the plodding succession of subjects and answers in the original fugue. Finally, he reduced the number of entrances and molded his composition into a more cohesive tonal structure.[2]

The bottom staves of fol. 33r have several sketches for three subjects and countersubjects in D, A, and F major. Two of these also appear in a separate autograph, which prompts a brief review of the chronology of Mendelssohn's

---

1. Cf. Marpurg's definition of the term (Mann, *Study of Fugue*, p. 155).
2. Except for one ill-timed entrance of the subject in A minor (m. 46).

fugues. On March 7, 1820, he completed a *Recitativo* for piano solo,[3] to which he added parts for violin, viola, and bass. His autograph string parts, all dated April 12, 1820, are preserved today in the Margaret Deneke Mendelssohn Collection at Oxford. On the reverse side of the viola part (shelfmark B. 5, fol. 199v), Zelter sketched in pencil the fugal subjects in D and F major which we find transferred to fol. 33r of the exercise book. The parts establish April 12, 1820, as a *terminus post quem* for Zelter's sketches. But this would seem too early, particularly since in April Mendelssohn was probably occupied with exercises in invertible counterpoint and since in May he was writing two-part canons (his diminution canon bears the date '25 Mai 20', for example). Presumably, Zelter registered his sketches on the viola part some time after April 12, perhaps toward the end of May, when Mendelssohn probably began his fugal studies.

Zelter's sketches from the autograph parts of April 12 are given in ex. 13. His primary purpose was to invent countersubjects suitable for invertible counterpoint. His choice of intervals, therefore, is marked by a prevailing number of thirds and sixths and a cautious employment of fifths. Mendelssohn copied these sketches, effected a few minor changes, and then selected the F major subject for his second two-part fugue (fol. 34r). He treated the opening exposition correctly by writing a real answer transposed a fifth above for the *comes*. But he was not consistent throughout: for example, the subject entries on E, B♭, and G (mm. 9, 19, and 29) are unconvincingly answered on C, A, and B♭ (mm. 14, 25, and 33).

Ex. 13
MDM B. 5 (fol. 199v)

The inexperienced student made some progress in his next exercise, a fugue in G major. Like its predecessor, this is prepared by a few sketches. First, the subject and countersubject were designed (fol. 32v), then the tonal answer (fol. 33v, foot; see p. 173). In other sketches of fol. 33v the subject and answer are combined in a stretto-like fashion, and the subject is placed alongside a new countersubject (not used by Mendelssohn, however, in the fugue). Mendelssohn's fugue based on this material (fols. 34v-35r) evinces a more promising and secure

3. For a facsimile, see Ranft, *Felix Mendelssohn Bartholdy*, Plate 4.

technique. It has five presentations of the subject and four intervening episodes with a clear tonal design:

I	vi	ii	IV	I
G	e	a	C	G
1	12	23	33	48

The two tonic statements form the endpoints of the movement; more remote key areas appear during the internal statements of the subject, while the sub-dominant passage articulates the return to the tonic.

What is surprising about these and the other two-part fugues is the scant evidence of Zelter's guiding hand – especially since guidance is in order. This contrasts strikingly with the 'ubiquitous' authority of the instructor in earlier sections of the workbook, particularly in the chorales. Zelter, it would seem, was content not to interfere with the novice's unsteady progress. This may have been judicious. There is at least one two-part fugue which bears little evidence of thorough revision and is altogether a considerably more sophisticated and reward-ing exercise. But Mendelssohn's success in this fugue in D minor (fol. 39v) may have been inspired by Bach, for it brings to mind the D minor fugue for three voices from the first volume of the *Well-Tempered Clavier* (ex. 14a). The two subjects share remarkably similar melodic constructions, even to the detail of an ornamental trill on their penultimate notes. Further, Bach answered the subject

Ex. 14a
Bach, BWV 851

Ex. 14b
Bach, BWV 851

Ex. 14c
Bach, BWV 851

at a fourth below, as did Mendelssohn. There are other less obvious points of comparison. Bach carefully integrated his subject into all aspects of the fugal structure. Thus, the countersubject contains in reverse order a diminished, abridged form of the principal subject (first six notes). From this descending pattern of the countersubject, in turn, he extracted an extended treatment of mirror inversion in the second half of the fugue (ex. 14b). Bach's fugue seems to thrive on any number of contrapuntal manipulations.

Mendelssohn's fugue, too, has a pronounced tendency toward elaborate linear relationships. The initial ascent of the subject is mimicked throughout by the constant, diminished motion of the countersubject in quavers (e.g. mm. 15-16). Toward the end, Mendelssohn associated fragments of the subject in quavers which are related by inversion (mm. 37ff.), creating an effect like the close of Bach's fugue (ex. 14c).

For his final two-part fugue, fittingly enough a setting of the *In secula seculorum amen*, Mendelssohn continued to amass various specialized contrapuntal techniques (fol. 40r). These include double counterpoint (mm. 15ff.), a combination of augmentation and stretto (mm. 23-28), and, at the conclusion, pedal point (mm. 37-40). The exercise is an effective summary of Mendelssohn's preliminary work with fugue.

9   Three-Part Fugue and Canon

In turning to three-part fugue, Mendelssohn was confronted by a new challenge, which Zelter would not have him take lightly. An ample supply of completed exercises, encompassing some eighteen fugues and several canons, rounds out the picture of the developing musician. While still laboring to refine his youthful fugal style, he did not hesitate to attempt intricate manipulations of his subjects. Indeed, it is as if the addition of a third contrapuntal part liberated numerous applications of diminution, augmentation, inversion, and stretto – devices that Fétis saw as appropriate for the relief of almost certain monotony and which Mendelssohn regarded as viable contrapuntal procedures.

These exercises, all written on three staves, are conceived for violin and piano. This we can determine, first, by the range of the upper part, which does not exceed a low G, and second, from the fact that these instruments are specifically indicated in two exercises (fols. 36v-37r; 42v-43r, mm. 38 and 49). We know that Felix took violin lessons as early as May, 1819, and by March, 1820, was diligently practicing Kreutzer studies. At his composition lessons Mendelssohn very likely performed the top part of his fugues on the violin, while Zelter played the lower two parts on the piano.

Some of the three-part fugues exist in separate, dated versions for solo organ. Here again we may use concordances, along with dated fugues in the workbook, to surmise a tentative chronology for the exercises. To begin with, two fugues are present as organ works in the *Mendelssohn Nachlass* in East Berlin. Mendelssohn's first three-part fugue, a *Largo* in D minor (fols. 27v-28r), is bound in the first volume of the collection after an unpublished Piano Sonata in A minor with the date May 12, 1820. In the workbook the fugue, out of sequence with the other three-part fugues, precedes Mendelssohn's diminution canon of May 25, 1820, and thus may be placed between these two dates. Another fugue (fols. 36v-37r) is found in the Berlin volume several folios after a *Presto* dated July 1, 1820, which may be accepted as a *terminus post quem*.

Several other three-voice fugues are more precisely dateable. Two (fols. 41v-42r, 50v-51r) open the second volume of Berlin autographs which Mendelssohn began to compile on December 3, 1820. Still another (fols. 61r-62r), recorded further on in the same volume, has the date January 5, 1821. Finally, Mendelssohn dated four more fugues, surviving only in the workbook, on January 17, 20, and 24,

1820, and on 'the 28th' (see the Inventory). There is a ready explanation for the unexpected incongruity of the year '1820'. Mendelssohn probably failed to remember that the year had changed (as he neglected to do in some of his letters from this time). If this was so, his three-part fugues may well belong to the period May, 1820, to January, 1821.

The conservative manner of Mendelssohn's training under Zelter is once again underlined in these exercises. Unconcerned by the current preoccupation with originality, Zelter grounded his instruction in the faithful imitation of approved eighteenth-century models. Mendelssohn's first fugue is a case in point (fols. 27v-28r). Its subject outlines the tonic and dominant degrees framed by the sixth and raised seventh degrees. A by-product is the interval of the diminished seventh, formed by the lowest and highest of the four pitches (m. 2). This kind of subject is a stock configuration of the eighteenth century. Fugal subjects with prominent diminished sevenths occur in numerous works by Bach and Handel, whose examples, in turn, were imitated by Haydn and Mozart.[1] Such a turning back to the past for models is, indeed, the outstanding characteristic of Zelter's tutelage, one which would profoundly influence Mendelssohn's mature outlook as well.

Three of Mendelssohn's fugues are coupled with brief preludes, a revival of a commonplace eighteenth-century scheme. Some of the preludes are based on contrapuntal techniques: the upper two voices of the D minor prelude, for example (fol. 36v), unfold in a canon at the unison. In the prelude of the Andante and Fugue in G minor (fols. 40v-42r) Mendelssohn manipulated two subjects in ingenious ways. The first motive is stated by the middle voice and imitated in a fugato-like texture at the fourth above and below (mm. 1-4). After inverting the upper two voices (mm. 5-7), Mendelssohn guided another entrance in the bass to a cadence on Bb major. This gives way in m. 11 to the second subject, also imitated fugally by the other voices. The dominant is attained in m. 17, and in the second part of the movement the subjects are now consolidated in various ways. In mm. 17-18, Mendelssohn placed them in the outer voices; in mm. 21-22, he juxtaposed the second subject with its mirror image; then he gave the first subject and its inversion to the outer voices, and the second subject to the middle voice. Finally, he completed his prelude with two alternative cadences: one a full close on the tonic, and the other a half-cadence on the dominant.

This experimentation with multiple subjects is carried over to the following Fugue in G minor (fols. 41v-42r): here Mendelssohn wrote a double fugue in which the subject and countersubject effectively exchange roles. That is to say, in the second half of the fugue the countersubject materializes as the subject of a new exposition while a portion of the original subject assumes the role of countersubject. Mendelssohn expended considerable effort on this scheme. First, though, he had to determine his answer and countersubject. In a two-staff sketch he tested a *comes* a fourth below the *dux* (fol. 41v). But, as he discovered, the literal

---

1. E.g., BWV 861, 865, 889, 1079; Handel's 'And with his stripes' from *Messiah*; Haydn's Op. 20, No. 5 (finale); and K 168 and 626.

transposition directed the answer to D minor, obliging him to compose a two-measure bridge back to the tonic for the third entrance. At this stage Zelter intervened: he retained almost intact the first three measures but entirely rewrote the fourth and invented for it a new motive consisting of quaver and two semiquavers (a double diminution of m. 1). Zelter's revised answer included a literal transposition of mm. 1-4, and an extension of one bar before the entrance of the third voice.

In the second portion of the fugue Mendelssohn indulged his penchant for advanced contrapuntal devices. After the reversal of subject and countersubject in m. 26, he reinstated the original subject (mm. 32-35) and set it simultaneously in diminution. Through this device the rhythmic values of the subject (minim and crotchets) and of Zelter's doubly diminished countersubject (quaver and semiquavers) were linked by a third level (crotchets and quavers). These metrical operations effectively injected a further degree of coherence into this already highly unified fugue.

Mendelssohn's third Prelude and Fugue (fols. 44v-46v) resuscitates a form outmoded by 1820 – it is unmistakably composed in the style of a French overture, inviting specific comparisons with various works of J. S. Bach and Handel. The very opening, a majestic exordium with ornamental flourishes, rapid scales in demisemiquavers, and a prolonged pedal point, is reminiscent of Bach's Partita in D major, BWV 828 (ex. 15a). In m. 2 Mendelssohn added figures, as if to clarify the implied voice leading above the pedal point; in the first measure of the Partita (second half) Bach had exploited the same basic motion of F♯, G, and A above the pedal. In several subsequent passages Mendelssohn reapplied the pedal point in a figure alternating between a diatonic line and a stationary pitch (e.g. mm. 4, 8-10) and yielding sequences of parallel tenths, or (under inversion) sixths, an ideal

Ex. 15a
Bach, BWV 828

Ex. 15b
Bach, BWV 884

Ex. 15c
after Zelter's sketch, Workbook, fol. 45v

pattern for three-part counterpoint. This had also been a favorite motive of J. S. Bach, as in his Prelude in G major from the second volume of the *Well-Tempered Clavier* (ex. 15b) or the elaborate harpsichord cadenza from the fifth *Brandenburg Concerto*.

As he did before, Mendelssohn equipped this prelude with a full cadence and an optional half-cadence, the latter intended as a link to the fugue. But he proceeded a step further by directly relating the fugue to the prelude. His sketches for the subject (fols. 44v, 45v) are very revealing: the first one is essentially a melodic reduction of the violin part from the opening of the prelude. Both begin with a leap from D to F♯ attended by a descent through an octave below. Perhaps the comparison was too obvious for Zelter, who produced a different form of the subject toward the bottom of the page. Nevertheless, Zelter's replacement barely masks an important thematic tie to the prelude. Considered together, the subject and answer unfold in a scale-like descent traversing the sixth D–F♯, an interval which relates by inversion to the ascending third D–F♯, the melodic kernel of the prelude (ex. 15c). Whether aware of this or not, Mendelssohn incorporated into his fugue at least two passages projecting similar descending scale motions (mm. 30-34, 42-46), and thereby further connected the movements. These carefully controlled relationships prove the youth to be an avid student of Bach's preludes and fugues, which are replete with complex thematic affinities between paired movements.[2]

Among Mendelssohn's three-part exercises are five canonic studies (fols. 55v-57r). They betray strong similarities to his earlier canons; in fact, two are two-part canons with an added free part for the violin. Occasionally this top part is imitative, as in the opening of the first canon. Typically, Mendelssohn resorted to well-tested melodic sequences on which to build his canons, as he had done previously. Of the three strict three-part ones, the first and third (fols. 56v, 57r) are the same except for a rearrangement of their voices. They are, however, flawed. In m. 7 of the first, for example, the exigencies of the canonic imitation led Mendelssohn to an improperly handled dissonant fourth. What is more, the inversion of the voices

2. Discussed, for example, in Keller, *Das wohltemperierte Klavier.*

(fol. 57r) created other predicaments, including an unmanageable $^6_4$ triad (m. 5), an unbecoming seventh (m. 6), and an ungraceful cadence on an inconclusive sixth chord (m. 8).

These canons, some of Mendelssohn's least successful exercises, are placed in the midst of his three-part fugues, as if a momentary respite from the youth's more serious endeavours. Two of the remaining three-part fugues, in A minor and C minor (fols. 62v-63v, 68v-70v), are more convincing. The subject of the A minor fugue is sketched on fol. 60r. Six measures in length, it divides into two sections demarcated by a quaver rest. A certain symmetry is achieved by the reiteration of the opening third A–B–C at the conclusion of the subject in its inverted and diminished form as C–B–A. Embedded in the sketch for the countersubject, too, are additional statements of the melodic third, as in m. 6, where Mendelssohn combined the two motives.

Strictly speaking, this fugue is bipartite in form; yet it shows incipient signs of a ternary design – enough, at least, for us to consider it a miniature three-part sonata movement. The first half has two fugal complexes on the tonic and mediant (mm. 1, 23), the second of which is prolonged to the cadence. After the double bar Mendelssohn turned to inverted forms of the subject, with entrances in G, C, and D in a development-like passage. In the third section, or reprise (m. 52), he artfully combined the original subject with its inversion at the same pitch level (and thus revived similar relationships in the opening exposition). He then contrived a stretto before a pedal point and final cadence. The exercise suggests, in short, a convincing synthesis of fugal elements and ternary form.

For his final three-part exercise (Plate V), Mendelssohn experimented with fugue within the most contrapuntal of the stylized baroque dance forms, the gigue (fols. 68v-70v). The complexities of his composition point again to Bach, particularly to the gigue-like fugues of the *Well-Tempered Clavier*.[3] Mendelssohn unveiled his subject, countersubject, and answer in a sketch which is placed several folios before this exercise (fol. 56r). His subject, a winding figure beginning on Ab, cleverly enough contains a portion of its own answer, a device Mendelssohn may have borrowed from Bach, who had exploited it in the second Bb major fugue from the *Well-Tempered Clavier* (ex. 16). It is driven by a three-note linear motive, present in both ascending and descending forms. These two forms recur in the countersubject, which, in fact, is largely a literal inversion of the subject. Characteristically, the fugue is full of involved, ingenious contrapuntal twists. Upon the completion of the exposition the fugue modulates to Eb major and the subject reappears in stretto between the lowest two voices. Mirror inversion follows (violin, m. 19), yielding in turn to combinations of the prime and inverted forms. Finally the subject is stated in augmentation (mm. 28-41) against an inversion in the bass.

Mendelssohn's gigue is the last entry in the exercise book; his next assignment, four-part fugue, is beyond the scope of the present study. But at least one three-

3. E.g., BWV 873, 880, and 887.

Plate V. Exercise book, fol. 68v

Ex. 16
Bach, BWV 890

part exercise in the workbook anticipates this next stage. In an incomplete draft of a fugue in C minor (fol. 66r-66v), an exposition for three voices (with another subject built on a diminished seventh) is extended by a fourth entry (m. 7), giving the illusion of an exposition with four statements, although the texture is limited to three voices. Mendelssohn, to be sure, did produce genuine four-part fugues. No fewer than twelve of them, dating from his thirteenth year (March–May, 1821) are dutifully written down in the second volume of the Berlin (DDR) autographs and still await publication.[4] And Felix was not the only member of the Mendelssohn family preoccupied with fugues: his sister Fanny, who as a teenager had mastered the *Well-Tempered Clavier*, was also immersed in them. Some three years later, indeed, Zelter could boast to the aging Goethe that she had just finished her thirty-second fugue![5]

Just consider how many times the principal subject must be heard in a fugue. If, in addition, it must be heard constantly in the same keys, whether in a higher or lower octave, with nothing else in between always in the same way, is it then possible to stifle one's disgust? Truly that is not the way the greatest fugue maker of our time, old Bach, thought. How many ingenious transpositions of the principal subject, how many splendidly assorted subsidiary ideas you will find there.[6]

Marpurg's tribute to Bach as a writer of fugues would have been appreciated by young Mendelssohn. In his studies he was stimulated by the potential for transforming and developing the fugal subject through specialized techniques. In this he was like Bach, who, according to Marpurg, 'shook all sorts of paper intricacies out of his sleeve'.[7] These exercises are indeed informed with the spirit of old Bach.

4. Examined in Friedrich, *Die Fugenkomposition*, pp. 25ff.
5. Geiger, *Briefwechsel* II, p. 298.
6. Marpurg, *Kritische Briefe* I, p. 266; trans. in David and Mendel, eds., *The Bach Reader*, p. 257.
7. *Ibid.*

10   Some Unknown *Juvenilia* of Mendelssohn

By January, 1821, as he filled the last few pages of his workbook with three-part fugues, Mendelssohn to his credit had finished an impressive number of compositions apart from his systematic schedule of exercises in figured bass, chorale, counterpoint, and fugue. As early as March, 1820, he had written his instrumental *Recitativo*, usually thought to be his first substantial composition. He soon tried his hand at a variety of instrumental and vocal compositions, including works for piano and organ, sonata-form movements for violin and piano and for piano solo, Lieder and part songs, sacred choral works, and dramatic scenes which were performed at the Mendelssohn residence in Berlin. A more ambitious undertaking was his first opera, the *Singspiel* entitled *Die Soldatenliebschaft*, finished by the end of 1820, and quickly followed by another, *Die beiden Pädagogen*, completed during the first three months of 1821.[1]

We can examine Mendelssohn's activity as a composer around this time through several previously unpublished compositions for piano solo and piano and violin which are scattered throughout the Oxford workbook. In the midst of the three-part exercises are two sets of variations, two movements in binary sonata form, and several miscellaneous pieces. These compositions, which rank among Mendelssohn's earliest completed works, present us with a stylistic dilemma. Some reveal fresh stylistic influences, as if Mendelssohn sought respite from the rigors of his fugal and canonic studies (and his association with the music of J. S. Bach). Others, replete with contrapuntal devices, bear the forceful mark of Zelter's systematic and traditional teaching. All are rooted in eighteenth-century practice; and not only Bach is invoked, but Haydn and Mozart are as well. Significantly, Mendelssohn does not yet seem to have come to terms with the music of Beethoven, Weber, Hummel, Field, or other contemporaries.

The two sets of variations, one in C major for piano and violin and one in D major for piano solo, are in particular heavily indebted to classical variation techniques. The theme of the first set (fols. 37v-39r) is a symmetrical structure of sixteen measures which subdivides into two halves and further into four four-measure phrases. Each phrase, in turn, breaks down into two-measure units, each introduced by an anacrusis of two quavers. The square and carefully balanced

---

1. Examined in Köhler, 'Zwei rekonstruierbare Singspiele'.

periodic structure and straightforward harmonic plan of the theme recall eight-eenth-century practice; particular details point convincingly to Haydn as a stylistic model. These include the recurring rhythmic motive ♩♩|♪♪♪♪|♩♩|♪♪ and the half-cadence in mm. 11-12, approached via a ii^6 harmony. Several Haydn themes with comparable stylistic features could be cited. One, displaying a similar periodic plan, an anacrusis of two quavers, and a half-cadence approached in the same manner, opens the Rondo finale to Haydn's Symphony No. 79 (ex. 17a).

Ex. 17a
Haydn, Symphony No. 79

Ex. 17b
Haydn, Hob. XVI: 48

The extent of Mendelssohn's debt to Haydn, though, is revealed by some strik-ing similarities to another theme, from the Rondo finale to the Sonata in C major for piano of 1790 (Hob. XVI: 48). The first half of Haydn's theme is presented in ex. 17b. It is in simple binary meter and begins with an anacrusis of two quavers.

It continues with a descending figure closely resembling m. 1 of Mendelssohn's theme (particularly if one disregards the two appoggiaturas in the Haydn excerpt). And Haydn's cadence (mm. 10-12), with its sliding chromatic lines of parallel sixths in the upper voices, was adapted by Mendelssohn in a diatonic version (the upper voice of the piano is doubled by the violin a sixth below). The evidence seems to point to a direct borrowing from Haydn; at the very least, Mendelssohn's theme suggests an intimate knowledge of Haydn's treatment of thematic and periodic construction.

Mendelssohn subjected his variations to a progressive series of rhythmic accelerations, another procedure derived from eighteenth-century practice. The first two variations employ an unbroken stream of semiquavers; the third and fourth introduce semiquaver triplets and demisemiquavers. Such systematic subdivisions of rhythmic values abound in the variations of Haydn, Mozart, and their contemporaries. It is found, for example, in the early quartets of Haydn (Op. 9, No. 5) and the piano trios (Hob. XV: 2), and in the Symphony No. 47 of 1772, which has the same succession of rhythmic adjustments as Mendelssohn's example. Rhythmic acceleration appears, too, in the well-known finales of Haydn's Quartet Op. 33, No. 5, and Mozart's Quartet, K 421. Indeed, Mendelssohn was not the only student composer to use this technique: Beethoven adopted it in an early work from the 1790s, the Piano Quartet in E♭ major (WoO 36, No. 1).

For the fifth and concluding variation of the set (mm. 81-110), Mendelssohn abandoned his scheme of rhythmic acceleration in favor of a rigid three-part fugato. It is as if the virtuoso display of the fourth variation is mitigated by a return to stark contrapuntal artistry – a move that is not at all surprising since these variations are surrounded in the workbook by two- and three-part fugues. For his subject Mendelssohn took the first two bars of the theme which he introduced in an initial exposition in all three voices. No fewer than ten additional entries appear in the remainder of the fugato, including statements of the subject on every melodic scale-degree except the leading-tone. The frequency of the entries and the skill with which they are applied bear ample testimony to his progress as a serious, if at times over-zealous, contrapuntist.

In the use of the violin, too, Mendelssohn is retrospective: on the whole, the violin is cast in a subordinate role to the piano, acting as an accompanying instrument rather than as an equal contributing partner. Only in the first variation (mm. 17-32) and in the concluding fugato, where the instrument's independence insures a three-part contrapuntal texture, does the violin emerge in a sustained solo capacity. More often than not, Mendelssohn observed in this work the eighteenth-century tradition of the accompanied keyboard sonata, as represented by many of Mozart's violin sonatas and the majority of Haydn's piano trios. (By the 1820s, however, largely due to the advances made by Beethoven in his violin and cello sonatas, that tradition was more or less obsolete.[2])

2. Though many nineteenth-century composers, such as Mendelssohn and Brahms, continued to assert the primacy of the piano part on the title pages of their chamber works.

Mendelssohn thus again appears to have been reared by Zelter primarily on eighteenth-century models; no signs of Beethoven's shattering impact or of the influence of other contemporary musicians disturb the studied symmetry of the C major variations. The second series of variations (fols. 53r-54r), for piano solo, shows further unmistakable references to the past. Again, Haydn looms as a prime stylistic source. In this case Mendelssohn used the so-called double-strophic variation form in which successive variations alternate between the tonic major and minor keys. He may have found precedents for the device in several of Haydn's instrumental compositions, such as the famous Divertimento in F minor (Hob. XVII: 6), the piano sonatas (Hob. XVI: 42 and 48), the string quartets (Op. 33, No. 6, Op. 50, No. 4, and Op. 54, No. 2), and the symphonies (Nos. 70, 82, and 103).[3]

Like the theme for the C major variations, Mendelssohn's D major melody is very Haydnesque. The first half, for example, yields fruitful comparisons with the opening measures of the well-known Rondo finale from the Quartet, Op. 74, No. 2 (ex. 18a). Some superficial similarities may be summarized: the two themes have the same time signature, begin with an anacrusis, and share a subdivision of the eight-measure period into two halves. More significantly, both appear in a high register, with chordal accompaniment in a middle range (Haydn omits the cello in his opening); their general contours are similar; and both make use of a quick harmonic progression, I–IV$^6_4$–I (Haydn, mm. 1-2; Mendelssohn, mm. 3-4). Rhythmically there are also further correlations, especially in the first four-measure phrase. Both composers wrote an unbroken succession of quavers, inter-

Ex. 18a
Haydn, Op. 74, No. 2

Ex. 18b
Haydn, Hob. XVI: 19

3. Mendelssohn also used the device in his F major Sonata for violin and piano, also from 1820, published as an advance release of *LA WFMB*, Ser. III, vol. V (Leipzig, 1977).

rupted only by semiquavers in the fourth measure to mark the articulation of the period into two halves. Whether or not Mendelssohn directly modeled his theme on the Haydn example remains speculative; nevertheless, the similarities noted here demonstrate again how thoroughly he assimilated and imitated Haydn's individual thematic construction. Haydn's influence is also evident further on in Mendelssohn's composition. The first D minor variation (mm. 17-32) borrows significantly from the finale of Haydn's Sonata in D major, Hob. XVI: 19. (Example 18b presents the first half of the D minor section from Haydn's finale.) The similarities between the two are too close to pass as mere coincidence. Each passage begins with a four-measure phrase descending by stepwise motion and doubled at the octave; each passage also displays in its second and third bars a prominent Bb auxiliary note with an embellishing trill.

In contrast to the jocose character of Haydn's finale, however, Mendelssohn's work soon adopts a more serious tone. After the unison beginning, the minor-key variation is abruptly transformed into a two-part canon at the octave. Further, the remaining minor-key variations, the third and fifth, are two-part canons at intervals of the third and fifth – as if Mendelssohn envisioned a kind of canonic cycle. The selected intervals of imitation – all drawn from the triad – seem to reflect the conspicuously triadic nature of the original theme. The structure of the entire composition may be conveniently schematized:

	Var. 1	Var. 2	Var. 3	Var. 4	Var. 5	Var. 6
Theme	Canon at 8	Theme	Canon at 3	Theme	Canon at 5	Theme
I	i	I	i	I	i	I

The three canons inject moments of contrapuntal complexity in contrast to the unassuming chordal structure of the theme – a theme which, as we have seen, might easily be mistaken for Haydn. The canons, perhaps, are designed as yet another methodical trial of Mendelssohn's contrapuntal acumen. Of the three, the third in particular is suspiciously academic. Its initial descending scale, in fact, is revived later in the workbook as the subject for a three-part fugue in D minor, which Mendelssohn recorded on fols. 61r-62r.

To conclude his second set of variations Mendelssohn created an elaborate cadential flourish which, like the series of canons, he fashioned to clash with the essentially Classical structure of the theme. Here he paid homage to J. S. Bach. In this closing (mm. 113-118) he embellished the dominant bass tone with an arpeggiated diminished-seventh chord built on G♯. The dissonant harmony resolves in m. 115 by a sudden leap to an A a seventh below. This registral displacement and the use of arpeggiation throughout the close bring to mind the conclusion of the C♯ major Prelude from the first volume of the *Well-Tempered Clavier* (ex. 18c).

The mixture of contrasting stylistic elements we have traced through the two sets of variations also characterizes other entries in the workbook, namely a group of four pieces for piano arranged as a suite, with alternating movements in the

Ex. 18c
Bach, BWV 848

tonic major and minor keys (fols. 43v-44v). The first movement, with its abundant embellishments, Alberti bass, and chromatic appoggiaturas, might easily be mistaken for an early work by Mozart. Ex. 19a offers the beginning of the Andante from the well-known Sonata, K 545. It parallels Mendelssohn's opening on several counts: along with the Alberti bass, the two four-measure phrases have a harmonic plan that unfolds over a tonic pedal point with a turn to the subdominant in m. 3 and a return to the tonic in m. 4; and each phrase concludes with an expressive chromatic dissonance, a C♯ doubled a tenth below by an A♯. (Mozart prepared the dissonance by descending stepwise motion; Mendelssohn, by leap.) Mendelssohn was not the only nineteenth-century composer to produce a melody similar to Mozart's. To our comparison may be added a third excerpt, from the Andante of Beethoven's Sonata, Op. 27, No. 1, which appears to borrow Mozart's harmonic plan (including the pedal point, though not the Alberti figuration) and chromatic dissonance doubled at the tenth (ex. 19b). Equally striking is the close thematic similarity between the Beethoven and Mendelssohn openings (especially mm. 2-4 of each example). Did Mendelssohn in 1820 imitate Beethoven's Sonata of 1801? One suspects not. The thematic resemblance might

Ex. 19a
Mozart, K 545

Ex. 19b
Beethoven, Op. 27, No. 1

be explained rather as a coincidental result of the two composers' independent imitation of Mozart's theme. The Alberti bass and the profusion of ornamental turns in Mendelssohn's melody suggests an eighteenth-century source; the noticeable lack of Beethoven's influence elsewhere in the Oxford workbook leads us to the same conclusion.

If Mendelssohn borrowed from Mozart in this cantabile theme, he also imitated Haydn. The beginning of the second half of the melody, which harmonically introduces V/ii and then ii before a half-cadence in m. 12, is characteristic of several themes by Haydn. A particularly appropriate comparison is afforded by a passage from the Minuet of the Sonata in B minor (Hob. XVI: 32, ex. 19c). (Note, for example, the expressive leaps of diminished sevenths in the two examples.)

Ex. 19c
Haydn, Hob. XVI: 32

Though Mendelssohn resorted to eighteenth-century models for the first movement of his suite, in the remaining movements he renewed his interest in counterpoint. The second and fourth movements are strict two-part canons at the octave. The third, a binary dance movement in common time, suggests a gavotte, though it is somewhat disguised by double counterpoint. All three demonstrate the youth's insatiable need to write counterpoint, a need we have observed in each of the compositions discussed so far. The canonic second movement, thematically related to the first, acts as a fulfilment of Mendelssohn's desire to test the contrapuntal potential of the G major melody. It begins with the same ornamental anacrusis, and its first four measures correspond roughly to the contour of the first four measures of the first movement. The second canon, the fourth movement of the suite (fol. 44v), also yields thematic analogies with the first movement, though the correspondences here are not as pronounced. The three are juxtaposed in ex. 19d, with melodic correspondences indicated by broken lines.

Ex. 19d

Ex. 19e
Bach, BWV 815

Mendelssohn did not extract thematic material from the first movement for the third movement of his suite. Like the second and fourth movements, however, the third movement is contrapuntally conceived. Though strict imitation is not applied throughout, it does begin with an ornament immediately imitated in the lower voice two octaves below and inverted in m. 5. The movement is liberally embellished with mordents; this and the emphasis on imitative writing are, again, derivative. It is not unlike the Gavotte from Bach's E♭ major French Suite (ex. 19e), which begins with a short motive in the upper voice subsequently imitated below.

The lavish embellishment and the double counterpoint are not the only retrospective features of this composition. In all probability Zelter intended Mendelssohn to write a gavotte in the eighteenth-century manner. Zelter himself had composed various dance pieces for Fasch as an introduction to the free style of composition;[4] in turn, Zelter prescribed the same course of instruction for his own pupils: for example, the exercise book of Gustav Wilhelm Teschner, who studied with him in 1825, is filled with minuets, polonaises, and gavottes.

For Teschner, Zelter cited portions of articles about such dances written by Kirnberger and J. A. P. Schulz for the encyclopaedic *Allgemeine Theorie der schönen Künste*, which began to appear under the editorship of Johann Georg

4. Schottländer, ed., *Carl Friedrich Zelters Darstellungen seines Lebens*, pp. 155-56.

Sulzer in 1771.[5] Here is the entry for the gavotte:

A short composition of reasonably cheerful and pleasant character intended for dancing. It is written in a measure of four even crotchets represented by ¢ in a meter of *alla breve* with two principal beats. It begins with an upbeat or in the second half of the measure on the third crotchet. It has segments of two measures which are extended always to the middle of the third measure:

The fastest notes are quavers. The complete piece divides into two parts, each with eight measures. But when the gavotte is intended not as a dance but as a keyboard piece or as part of a suite, one need not be confined to this length.[6]

Mendelssohn, to be sure, did not produce a gavotte *à la* Kirnberger, though he incorporated into his piece – no doubt with Zelter's encouragement – certain features of the description. His movement begins with an upbeat; it uses primarily an even succession of crotchets (more evident if one takes into account the steady exchange between the two voices); its fastest values are quavers; and it divides into two parts, the first with eight measures, the second an elongated section of twelve measures, as permitted by Kirnberger. Finally, the frequent rests and the contour of the melody imply an *alla breve* meter, even though Mendelssohn specified common time. But apart from these features, the movement is regulated by imitation and double counterpoint – elements that once again seem to pre-empt other musical considerations.

Only in one composition in the workbook, a ternary-form movement for violin and piano (fols. 42v-43r, Plate VI), did Mendelssohn manage without any involved contrapuntal writing. Much of this scherzo-like movement mimics Haydn's jocose musical vocabulary. For example, Mendelssohn playfully experimented with registral leaps in mm. 21-25, a prime technique encountered in Haydn's music.[7] In the central section in G major, marked by a shift to a running triplet figuration shared by both instruments, one passage (mm. 46-50) includes a harmonic pattern frequently used by Haydn and already observed in Mendelssohn's G major theme for piano solo (cf. ex. 19c). But even in the G minor movement for piano and violin Mendelssohn could not completely suppress his contrapuntal urges. Thus, in m. 5 he inverted the opening violin melody to the bass; on occasion he even fashioned accompaniments in almost strict inversion to the melody, as in the piano part of mm. 26-27 or 50-53. In summary, the movement has the now familiar mixture of classical stylistic traits and didactic influences.

The two monothematic sonata movements for violin and piano, an Andante in D minor (fols. 51v-52v) and an Allegro in C major (fols. 57v-58v), are especially conservative. The first opens with a lengthy, ten-measure subject answered a fifth above by the violin in m. 11, as if to suggest a fugue rather than a sonata move-

5. Described in detail in Seaton, 'A Composition Course with Carl Friedrich Zelter', pp. 132-38.
6. Sulzer, ed., *Allgemeine Theorie* II, p. 309.
7. E.g., the finales of Op. 33, No. 3; Op. 64, No. 2; and Hob. XVI:43.

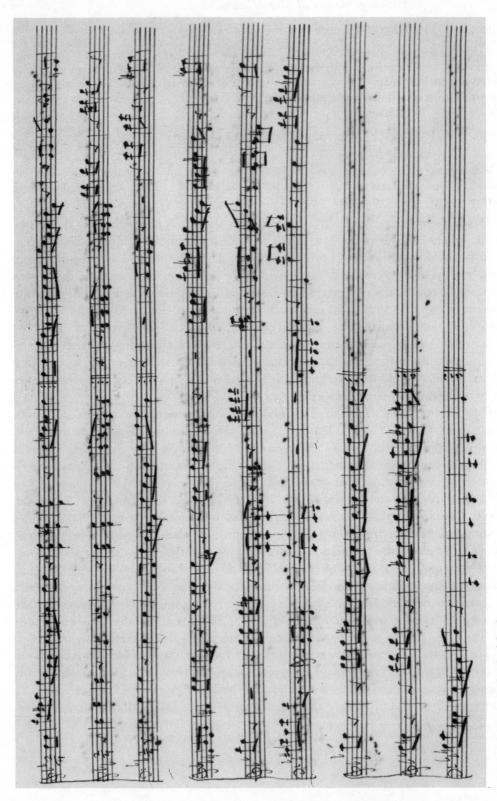

Plate VI. Exercise book, fol. 42v

ment. The layered rhythmic texture of continuous semiquavers over the motion of the bass in quavers, and the descending sequence in mm. 4-5 are striking stylistic references to the early eighteenth century. The broken arpeggiated figure of mm. 6-7 vividly recalls Bach's well-known *Inventio* in A minor (ex. 20a), and the third movement from Handel's Suite in G minor (ex. 20b). Equally striking, though, is the use of contrapuntal manipulations – already well rehearsed in the exercises and now applied once again in this early composition. Thus, in the second half of the movement the subject is introduced in inversion by the violin and answered by the piano. And at the end of the work, the original and inverted forms are superimposed over a tonic pedal point (mm. 81ff.). Similarly, the subject of Mendelssohn's C major Allegro (fol. 57v) appears throughout the movement in both imitation (mm. 16-17, 35-39, 42-58) and diminution (mm. 62-64), further illustrating the boy's contrapuntal ingenuity. This preoccupation with abstruse techniques evidently bears witness to Mendelssohn's industrious study of counterpoint, and to Zelter's influence upon him.

Ex. 20a
Bach, BWV 784

Ex. 20b
Handel, Suite in G minor

In terms of their form, Mendelssohn's two sonata movements of 1820 are reactionary. Sonata form is represented here as a binary or rudimentary ternary structure, nothing at all like the mature sonata movements of Haydn and Mozart (recognized in the nineteenth century by such theorists as Anton Reicha, Carl Czerny, and A. B. Marx). The D minor movement divides into two nearly equal parts, of 41 and 44 bars. In the C major movement, Mendelssohn actually repeated both portions and thus emphasized their binary division. The pervasive monothematicism, as well, seems to show the influence of a considerably earlier age. Evidently by 1820, the eleven-year-old Mendelssohn had not fully grasped the significance of the work of Beethoven, Dussek, Hummel, or Weber.

In many ways, these two compositions expose the novice struggling to acquire mastery of form. Mendelssohn evidently found the area immediately after the exposition in each movement especially troublesome. What development there is is largely a result of contrived passage work and sequence, which are not always entirely convincing. In the development of the D minor movement, for example, Mendelssohn began with the inversion of the first theme in the mediant, F major. This is sequentially repeated in the piano one step above in G minor (m. 51); eight measures later, however, the mediant is tautologically regained. In the next few measures Mendelssohn quickly moved by chromatic motion in the bass to the dominant (mm. 61-65) and introduced the reprise shortly thereafter. The entire section functions more as a transition than a development. In the C major movement Mendelssohn began his development with a passage in stretto but almost immediately returned to the tonic (m. 40). He then attempted a new modulatory passage, but ended it, too, in C major. In each case Mendelssohn departed from the tonic only to return to it prematurely.

The two sonata movements thus reveal an inexperience with sonata form. Eighteenth-century binary form is exhumed in these youthful essays, principally because Mendelssohn had not matured enough to grasp the significance of later developments in sonata form; it may be, too, that Zelter insisted upon a fairly constrained and traditional approach to composition. Mendelssohn's encounter with extended sonata form, however, was not delayed much longer. Later in 1820, he produced more substantial sonata-form works with more ambitious development sections, as the little-known F major Sonata for violin and piano demonstrates.[8] Nevertheless, he still continued to avoid thematic contrast in his sonata-form movements. Monothematicism prevails in the F major Violin Sonata, the one-movement Sonata in B♭ minor for piano from 1823,[9] the Overture to *Die beiden Pädagogen* (1821), the Piano Quartet, Op. 2 (also from 1823), and the two posthumous sonatas in G minor and B♭ major for piano (Opp. 105 and 106, completed in 1821 and 1827).

The various compositions in the workbook represent, of course, only a portion of Mendelssohn's output during 1820 and 1821, much of which still awaits publication. The dependence of these early works on eighteenth-century models is typical of the other music he wrote at this time. In 1821 he began a series of thirteen *sinfonie* scored for strings alone, primarily with a division of the orchestra into four parts.[10] These works are strongly indebted to the string symphonies of C. P. E. Bach and other north German eighteenth-century composers; in addition, one can find in them examples of the French overture, several fugues on chromatic subjects, and double fugues. In other works Mendelssohn borrowed rather directly from eighteenth-century masters. In 1823 he finished a set of variations for organ on the chorale 'Wie groß ist des Allmächt'gen Güte', clearly intended as an homage to J. S. Bach: the second variation, for example, displays the chorale in a series of canons at the octave, fourth, and third, and modestly recalls Bach's

---

8. See n. 3 above.
9. See Todd, 'A Sonata by Mendelssohn'.
10. He rescored the eighth separately for full orchestra; he eventually released the thirteenth, also for full orchestra, as his First Symphony, Op. 11.

canonic *tour de force* on 'Vom Himmel hoch'. In the finale to the *Singspiel, Die beiden Pädagogen*, on the other hand, Mendelssohn borrowed from Mozart: he set the principal soloists against a chorus of peasants by juxtaposing two conflicting meters, a technique reminiscent of Mozart's famous polymetrical experiment in Act I of *Don Giovanni*. Finally, in the last movement of the F major Violin Sonata, he constructed a theme suspiciously similar to the opening of the *Vivace* from Haydn's Symphony No. 102 in B♭ major (exx. 21a and b).

Ex. 21a
Haydn, Symphony No. 102

Ex. 21b
Mendelssohn, Violin Sonata in F major

Mendelssohn's music from the early 1820s also displays at times a stark, didactic character – again an unmistakable sign of Zelter's influence. The lessons of the composition workbook are put to the test on numerous occasions. Thus, the chorale variations on 'Wie groß ist des Allmächt'gen Güte', in addition to recalling the attempted canonic cycle in the D major variations (fols. 53r-54r), bring to mind the chorale exercises: the cantus firmus appears in the opening movement in the bass and is transposed to the soprano in the third movement, where it is adorned with prolific embellishment in the manner of Kirnberger's *verziehrter Contrapunkt*. Many of Mendelssohn's other works contain elaborate, sometimes arbitrary, contrapuntal passages. For example, the development of the first movement of the posthumous G minor Piano Sonata, Op. 105, is interrupted to permit a brief two-part canon which leads, somewhat unconvincingly, to a false reprise (ex. 22). Further on in the movement, Mendelssohn devised a passage in invertible counterpoint (ex. 23), while in the F major Violin Sonata he treated a theme in mirror inversion (ex. 24) in a spirit recalling his three-part fugues (for instance the Fugue in A minor, fols. 62v-63v, or the Andante in D minor for violin and piano, fols. 51v-52v). In short, there are no signs in the works of the early 1820s of departure from the styles of the traditional exercises and compositions of the workbook. Rather, these were years of consolidation for Mendelssohn as he attempted to apply to his maturing art the principles he had learned during his studies with Zelter.

Ex. 22
Mendelssohn, Sonata, Op. 105

Ex. 23
Mendelssohn, Sonata, Op. 105

Ex. 24
Mendelssohn, Violin Sonata in F major

11 Summary

Exactly when Mendelssohn concluded his formal lessons with Zelter cannot be determined. The exercises in the workbook were followed in 1821 by several four-part fugues;[1] these and the series of string *sinfonie*, which were performed privately at the Mendelssohn household, represented the culmination of Zelter's instruction. In 1824, at a celebration after the performance of the prodigy's fourth opera, *Die beiden Neffen*, Zelter proudly took the opportunity to proclaim that his pupil was a mature musician who could rightfully join the brotherhood of Sebastian Bach, Haydn, and Mozart. Judging from Mendelssohn's early compositions, we can readily appreciate the appropriateness of Zelter's selection of composers. By 1820, Mendelssohn was thoroughly engrossed by the music of these eighteenth-century masters; by 1824 - only one year before the Octet, the finale of which effectively represents the summation of his mastery of counterpoint - he had acquired a remarkable technical proficiency and creative maturity.

Why Zelter in 1824 ignored such contemporary musicians as Beethoven and Weber is a vexing question; there can be no doubt, however, that by 1824 Mendelssohn was thoroughly acquainted with the important music of his own day - largely because of several important new musical experiences. In June, 1821, only a few months after the completion of his composition workbook with Zelter, he had attended the premiere of *Der Freischütz* in Berlin, which polarized the audience into rival Spontini and Weber factions, the one reactionary, the other romantically iconoclastic. The powerful influence of Weber's score would be felt in the first movement of Mendelssohn's Symphony in C minor, Op. 11. By 1824, the year of the Symphony, Mendelssohn had associated with Hummel and Moscheles, the former during Mendelssohn's visit to Goethe in Weimar during 1821. Not surprisingly, stylistic traces of the music of these and other virtuosi began to appear in Mendelssohn's piano works and concerti from this time. His first serious assimilation of Beethoven's music appears to date from 1823: the finale of the A♭ major Concerto for two pianos, completed in 1823, shows the influence of the finale of Beethoven's Third Piano Concerto[2] (though a likely model was the genuinely romantic Concerto in A♭ major by John Field). In 1826, Mendelssohn was to compose a B♭ major Piano Sonata (Op. 106) reminiscent of

1. See Chap. 9, n. 4.
2. Discussed in Todd, 'Instrumental Music', pp. 358f.

84

the 'Hammerklavier' Sonata;[3] only the year before, while in Paris, he had lamented the French ignorance of *Fidelio*. The years immediately following the completion of the exercise book in 1821, then, were decisive ones for Mendelssohn's musical development.

Clearly the handful of compositions in the workbook directly precedes such a sudden burst of creative development. They bear the unavoidable imprint of the didactic exercises which surround them; and, to be sure, they reflect for 1820 and 1821 a narrow musical environment – imposed, one suspects, by Zelter's reactionary teaching. This, though, does not detract from their value as an important record of the development of a musical prodigy. These compositions, unabashedly grounded in eighteenth-century practice, display Mendelssohn's remarkable reverence for musical tradition.

This reverence, in the final analysis, was Zelter's chief legacy to Mendelssohn, who as a mature musician embraced the musical past in many ways. Most obviously, he continued to practice and refine his skill in the academic forms of his student exercises – thoroughbass, chorale, canon, and fugue. He used figured bass as a shorthand device in his sketches and included continuo parts in several of his sacred works, the *Ave Maria*, Op. 23, No. 2,[4] and Psalm 42, Op. 42, among them. His later devotion to the chorale may only be described as a preoccupation with the form. Chorales, whether freely composed or drawn from the traditional repertory, permeate nearly every type of composition he undertook, from the organ sonata, piano trio (e.g. Op. 66) and symphony (e.g. the 'Lobgesang' and 'Reformation' symphonies) to the oratorio, chorale cantata, and even the incidental music to Racine's *Athalia*. Similarly, like Brahms and Reger, Mendelssohn was strongly attracted to canon and fugue. Throughout his career, he produced presentation canons[5] almost as a measure of self-discipline, and, of course, as a reflection of his study with Zelter. More substantial canons appear in a variety of compositions such as the String Quintet, Op. 18;[6] *Lerchengesang*, Op. 48, No. 4; Psalm 95, Op. 46; and the March, Op. 108. Representative fugues may be found in the string quartets, Opp. 12 and 13; Octet, Op. 20; preludes and fugues, Opp. 35 and 37; and *St Paul* and *Elijah*, to name only a few works. Finally, signs of Mendelssohn's childhood labors in counterpoint re-emerge in his instinctive, at times seemingly overbearing, need to vitalize the thematic material of any number of compositions with contrapuntal elaborations.[7]

3. See Newman, 'Some 19th-Century Consequences'.
4. For the first version (1830) he provided only an unrealized figured bass line for the continuo – at a time when figured bass was rapidly becoming obsolete; for the second he was more practical, providing a choice between a fully realized continuo part for organ and, for performances without organ, a realization for clarinets, bassoons, and strings.
5. For a list of thirty-six, see Todd, 'Instrumental Music', pp. 127-30.
6. In the rejected Minuet from the first version; several detailed sketches for the canonic Trio survive. See *ibid.* pp. 308-22.
7. As in the *Hebrides* Overture, and the rejected Symphony in C major and Piano Concerto in E minor, discussed in Todd, 'Of Sea Gulls and Counterpoint', 'An Unfinished Symphony', and 'An Unfinished Piano Concerto'.

Beyond this, Zelter's influence is reflected in Mendelssohn's unwavering interest in the past, and his desire to promote rather than neglect its musical treasures – his well-known efforts to cultivate the music of Bach and Handel are two notable expressions of that attitude. Ironically, Zelter expressed on at least one occasion his concern for Mendelssohn's zealous emulation of earlier music. Toward the end of 1830, when Mendelssohn traveled to Rome and composed en route several conservative sacred works, the aging Zelter wrote to his former pupil and admonished him against excessive imitation of eighteenth-century masters. In his reply Mendelssohn sought to allay Zelter's fears:

In your last letter you seemed anxious lest, following my predilection for one of the great masters, I might devote myself too much to church music and be led into imitation. Such, however, is certainly not the case . . . Naturally, nobody can forbid me to enjoy the inheritance left by the great masters nor to continue to work at it, because not everybody has to begin at the beginning. But then it must be continued creation according to one's ability, and not a lifeless repetition of what is already there.[8]

Clearly Mendelssohn viewed his music as an act of 'continuing creation', not simply one of deference to the past. Nevertheless, his respect for the authority of musical tradition, so clearly documented by the exercise book, played a prominent role in his continuing championship of earlier music and, indeed, always influenced profoundly the nature of his own work.

8. Mendelssohn, *Letters*, pp. 105-6.

Select Bibliography

Abraham, Gerald, 'Weber as Novelist and Critic', *MQ* XX (1934), pp. 27-38

Allgemeine musikalische Zeitung, ed. F. Rochlitz (Leipzig, 1798-1819)

Bach, C. P. E., *Essay on the True Art of Playing Keyboard Instruments*, ed. and trans. W. J. Mitchell (N. Y., 1949)

Beach, D. W., 'The Harmonic Theories of Johann Philipp Kirnberger: Their Origins and Influence' (Diss., Yale Univ., 1974)

Berliner allgemeine musikalische Zeitung, ed. A. B. Marx (Berlin, 1824-1830)

Berlioz, Hector, *Correspondance générale*, ed. Pierre Citron, I (Paris, 1972)

The Memoirs of Hector Berlioz, ed. and trans. David Cairns (N. Y., 1975)

Besseler, Heinrich, 'Bach als Wegbereiter', *AfMw* XII (1955), pp. 1-39

Blume, Friedrich, 'Bach in the Romantic Era', *MQ* L (1964), pp. 290-306

Bononcini, G. M., *Musico prattico* (Bologna, 1673; rep. Hildesheim, 1969)

Bruckner, Anton, *Vorlesungen über Harmonielehre und Kontrapunkt*, ed. E. Schwanzara (Vienna, 1950)

Caldara, Antonio, *Ein Madrigal und achtzehn Kanons*, ed. Karl Geiringer, in *Das Chorwerk* XXV (Wolfenbüttel, 1933)

Crum, Margaret, ed., *Felix Mendelssohn Bartholdy* (Oxford, 1972)

Dahlhaus, Carl, ed., *Das Problem Mendelssohn* (Regensburg, 1974)

David, H. T., and Mendel, Arthur, eds., *The Bach Reader*, rev. ed. (N. Y., 1966)

Devrient, Eduard, *My Recollections of Felix Mendelssohn-Bartholdy, and his Letters to Me*, trans. N. Macfarren (London, 1869; rep. N. Y., 1972)

Elvers, Rudolf, 'Verzeichnis der von Felix Mendelssohn Bartholdy herausgegebenen Werke Johann Sebastian Bachs', *Gestalt und Glaube: Festschrift für Oskar Söhngen* (Berlin, 1960), pp. 145-49

'Ein Jugendbrief von Felix Mendelssohn', *Festschrift für Friedrich Smend zum 70. Geburtstag* (Berlin, 1963), pp. 95-97

'Ein nicht abgesandter Brief Zelters an Haydn', *Musik und Verlag: Karl Vötterle zum 65. Geburtstag am 12. April 1968*, ed. Richard Baum and Wolfgang Rehm (Kassel, 1968), pp. 243-45

'Verzeichnis der Musik-Autographen von Fanny Hensel im Mendelssohn-Archiv zu Berlin', *MS* I (1972), pp. 169-74

'Weitere Quellen zu den Werken von Fanny Hensel', *MS* II (1975), pp. 215-20

Fétis, F.-J., *Traité du contrepoint et de la fugue* (Paris, 1824; rep. Osnabrück, 1972)

Filosa, A. J., 'The Early Symphonies and Chamber Music of Felix Mendelssohn Bartholdy' (Diss., Yale Univ., 1970)

Forkel, J. N., *Über Johann Sebastian Bachs Leben, Kunst, und Kunstwerke* (Leipzig, 1802; rep. Kassel, 1942); trans. C. S. Terry as *Johann Sebastian Bach, his Life, Art and Work* (London, 1920)

Friedrich, Gerda, *Die Fugenkomposition in Mendelssohns Instrumentalwerk* (Bonn, 1969)

Fux, J. J., *Gradus ad Parnassum* (Vienna, 1725)
   The Study of Counterpoint, trans. Alfred Mann (N. Y., 1965)

Geck, Martin, *Die Wiederentdeckung der Matthäuspassion* (Regensburg, 1967)

Geiger, Ludwig, ed., *Briefwechsel zwischen Goethe und Zelter*, 3 vols. (Leipzig, 1902)

Gellert, C. F., *Sämmtliche Schriften*, II (Leipzig, 1769; rep. Hildesheim, 1968)

Gilbert, Felix, ed., *Bankiers, Künstler und Gelehrte: unveröffentlichte Briefe der Familie Mendelssohn aus dem 19. Jahrhundert* (Tübingen, 1975)

Grant, C. P., 'The Real Relationship between Kirnberger's and Rameau's Concept of the Fundamental Bass', *JMT* XXI (1977), pp. 324-38

Großmann-Vendrey, Susanna, 'Die Orgelwerke von Felix Mendelssohn Bartholdy' (Diss., Univ. of Vienna, 1965)
   Felix Mendelssohn Bartholdy und die Musik der Vergangenheit (Regensburg, 1969)

Händel, G. F., *Aufzeichnungen zur Kompositionslehre*, ed. Alfred Mann, in *Hallische Händel-Ausgabe*, Supplement, I (Kassel, 1978)

Helm, Eugene, *Music at the Court of Frederick the Great* (Norman, Oklahoma, 1960)

Hensel, Sebastian, ed., *Die Familie Mendelssohn 1729-1847*, 3 vols. (Berlin, 1879); trans. Carl Klingemann as *The Mendelssohn Family (1729-1847)*, 2 vols. (N. Y., 1882)

Hiller, Ferdinand, *Felix Mendelssohn-Bartholdy: Briefe und Erinnerungen* (Cologne, 1874); trans. M. E. von Glehn (London, 1874)

Hiller, J. A., *Fünf und zwanzig neue Choralmelodien zu Liedern von Gellert* (Leipzig, 1792)

Hiller, J. A., ed., *Wöchentliche Nachrichten und Anmerkungen die Musik betreffend* (Leipzig, 1766-70; rep. Hildesheim, 1970)

Irmen, Hans-Josef, ed., *Engelbert Humperdinck als Kompositionsschüler Josef Rheinbergers*, 2 vols. (Cologne, 1974)

Jacobi, E. R., 'Das Autograph von C. Ph. E. Bachs Doppelkonzert in Es-dur für Cembalo, Fortepiano und Orchester (Wq. 47, Hamburg, 1788)', *Mf* XII (1959), pp. 488-89
   'C. F. Zelters kritische Beleuchtung von J. N. Forkels Buch über J. S. Bach, aufgrund neu aufgefundener Manuskripte', *International Musicological*

Society, *Report of the Eleventh Congress*, ed. Henrik Glahn, Søren Sørensen, and Peter Ryom (Copenhagen, 1974) II, pp. 462-66

Keil, Siegmar, *Untersuchungen zur Fugentechnik in Robert Schumanns Instrumentalschaffen* (Hamburg, 1973)

Keller, Hermann, *Das wohltemperierte Klavier von J. S. Bach* (Kassel, 1965)

'Johann Adolf Scheibe und Johann Sebastian Bach', *Musik und Verlag: Karl Vötterle zum 65. Geburtstag*, ed. Richard Baum and Wolfgang Rehm (Kassel, 1968), pp. 383-86

Kircher, Athanasius, *Musurgia universalis* (Rome, 1650; rep. Hildesheim, 1970)

Kirkendale, Warren, 'The "Great Fugue" Op. 133: Beethoven's "Art of Fugue"', *Acta* XXXV (1963), pp. 14-24

Fuge und Fugato in der Kammermusik des Rokoko und der Klassik (Tutzing, 1966; rev., trans., Durham, North Carolina, 1979)

Kirnberger J. P., *Die Kunst des reinen Satzes in der Musik*, 2 vols. (Berlin, 1771-79; rep. Hildesheim, 1968)

Grundsätze des Generalbasses als erste Linien zur Composition (Berlin, 1781; rep. Hildesheim, 1974)

Gedanken über die verschiedenen Lehrarten in der Komposition, als Vorbereitung zur Fugenkenntniss (Berlin, 1782; rep. Hildesheim, 1974)

Klingemann, Karl, ed., *Felix Mendelssohn-Bartholdys Briefwechsel mit Legationsrat Karl Klingemann in London* (Essen, 1909)

Köhler, Karl-Heinz, 'Zwei rekonstruierbare Singspiele von Felix Mendelssohn Bartholdy', *BzM* II/3-4 (1960), pp. 86-93

'Das Jugendwerk Felix Mendelssohns: die vergessene Kindheitsentwicklung eines Genies', *DJdM* VII (1962), pp. 18-35

Kollmann, A. F. C., *A Practical Guide to Thorough-Bass* (London, 1801)

Kramer, Richard, 'Notes to Beethoven's Education, *JAMS* XXVIII (1975), pp. 72-101

Krummacher, Friedhelm, *Mendelssohn, der Komponist: Studien zur Kammermusik für Streicher* (Munich, 1978)

Lach, Robert, *W. A. Mozart als Theoretiker* (Vienna, 1918)

Lindblad, A. F., *Bref till Adolf Fredrik Lindblad från Mendelssohn, Dohrn, Almquist, Atterbom, Geijer, Fredrika Bremer, C. W. Böttiger, och andra*, ed. L. Dahlgren (Stockholm, 1913)

Mann, Alfred, *The Study of Fugue*, 2nd ed. (N. Y., 1965)

'Eine Kompositionslehre von Händel', *HJ 1964/65* (1965), pp. 35-57

'Beethoven's Contrapuntal Studies with Haydn', *MQ* LVI (1970), pp. 711-26

'Haydn as Student and Critic of Fux', *Studies in Eighteenth-Century Music: a Tribute to Karl Geiringer on his Seventieth Birthday*, ed. H. C. R. Landon (N. Y., 1970), pp. 323-32

'Haydn's Elementarbuch: A Document of Classic Counterpoint Instruction', *The Music Forum* III (1973), pp. 197-237

'Zu Schuberts Studien im strengen Satz', *Schubert-Kongreß Wien 1978:*

Bericht, ed. Otto Brusatti (Graz, 1979), pp. 127-39

Marpurg, F. W., *Die Abhandlung von der Fuge* (Berlin, 1753-54; rep. Hildesheim, 1970)

Kritische Briefe über die Tonkunst, 2 vols. (Berlin, 1760; rep. Hildesheim, 1974)

Marshall, Robert, 'How J. S. Bach Composed Four-Part Chorales', *MQ* LVI (1970), pp. 198-220

Marx, A. B., *Die Lehre von der musikalischen Komposition* (Leipzig, 1837-47); trans. A. Wehran as *The School of Musical Composition* (London, 1852)

Mekeel, Joyce, 'The Harmonic Theories of Kirnberger and Marpurg', *JMT* IV (1960), pp. 169-93

Mendelssohn Bartholdy, Felix, *Briefe aus den Jahren 1830 bis 1847*, ed. Paul Mendelssohn Bartholdy, 2 vols. (Leipzig, 1863-64)

Briefe an Ignaz und Charlotte Moscheles, ed. Felix Moscheles (Leipzig, 1888); trans. Felix Moscheles (Boston, 1888)

Letters, ed. and trans. G. Selden-Goth (N. Y., 1945)

Leipziger Ausgabe der Werke Felix Mendelssohn Bartholdys (Leipzig, 1960-)

Paphlëis: ein Spott-Heldengedicht, ed. M. F. Schneider and Ursula Galley (Basle, 1961)

Briefe an deutsche Verleger, ed. Rudolf Elvers (Berlin, 1968)

Briefe aus Leipziger Archiven, ed. Hans-Joachim Rothe and Reinhard Szeskus (Leipzig, 1972)

O Haupt voll Blut und Wunden, ed. R. Larry Todd (Madison, 1981)

Mendelssohn Bartholdy, Karl, *Goethe und Felix Mendelssohn Bartholdy* (Leipzig, 1871); trans. M. E. von Glehn as *Goethe and Mendelssohn* (London, 1874)

Milz, Friedemann, *A-cappella-Theorie und musikalischer Humanismus bei August Eduard Grell* (Regensburg, 1976)

Mintz, Donald, 'Some Aspects of the Revival of Bach', *MQ* XL (1954), pp. 201-21

Mitchell, W. J., 'Chord and Context in 18th-Century Theory', *JAMS* XVI (1963), pp. 221-39

Moscheles, Ignaz, *Recent Music and Musicians*, trans. A. D. Coleridge (N. Y., 1874)

Mozart, W. A., *Thomas Attwoods Theorie- und Kompositionsstudien bei Mozart*, ed. Erich Hertzmann, C. B. Oldman, Alfred Mann, and Daniel Heartz, in *Neue-Mozart-Ausgabe*, XXX/1 (Kassel, 1965)

Neumann, Werner, 'Welche Handschriften J. S. Bachscher Werke besaß die Berliner Singakademie?', *Hans Albrecht in Memoriam*, ed. Wilfried Brennecke and Hans Haase (Kassel, 1962), pp. 136-42

Newman, W. S., 'Some 19th-Century Consequences of Beethoven's "Hammerklavier" Sonata, Op. 106', *PQ* LXVIII (1969), pp. 12-17

The Sonata Since Beethoven (N. Y., 1972)

Nottebohm, Gustav, ed., *Beethoven's Studien, erster Band: Beethoven's Unterricht bei J. Haydn, Albrechtsberger, und Salieri* (Leipzig, 1873)

Rameau, Jean-Philippe, *Treatise on Harmony*, trans. Philip Gossett (N. Y., 1971)

Ranft, Peter, *Felix Mendelssohn Bartholdy: eine Lebenschronik* (Leipzig, 1972)

Revitt, P. J., 'Domenico Corri's "New System" for Reading Thoroughbass', *JAMS* XXI (1968), pp. 93-98

Roesner, Linda, 'Studies in Schumann Manuscripts with Particular Reference to Sources Transmitting Instrumental Works in the Large Forms', 2 vols. (Diss., New York Univ., 1973)

Scheibe, J. A., *Critischer Musikus* (Leipzig, 1745; rep. Hildesheim, 1970)

Schering, Arnold, 'Joh. Phil. Kirnberger als Herausgeber Bachscher Choräle', *BJ 1918* (1919), pp. 141-50

Schneider, Max, 'Verzeichnis der bis zum Jahre 1851 gedruckten (und der geschrieben im Handel gewesenen) Werken von Johann Sebastian Bach', *BJ 1906* (1907), pp. 84-113

Schöne, Alfred, and Hiller, Ferdinand, eds., *The Letters of a Leipzig Cantor, Being the Letters of Moritz Hauptmann to Franz Hauser, Ludwig Spohr, and Other Musicians*, trans. A. D. Coleridge, 2 vols. (London, 1879)

Schottländer, J. W., ed., *Carl Friedrich Zelters Darstellungen seines Lebens*, in *Schriften der Goethe Gesellschaft* XLIV (Weimar, 1931)

Schubring, Julius, ed., *Briefwechsel zwischen Felix Mendelssohn Bartholdy und Julius Schubring* (Leipzig, 1892)

Schulze, Hans-Joachim, '"Das Stück in Goldpapier": Ermittlungen zu einigen Bach-Abschriften des frühen 18. Jahrhunderts', *BJ 1978* (1978), pp. 19-42

Schumann, Clara, *Jugendbriefe von Robert Schumann* (Leipzig, 1898)

Schumann, Robert, *Erinnerungen an Felix Mendelssohn Bartholdy*, ed. Georg Eismann (Zwickau, 1948)

Schünemann, Georg, 'Mendelssohns Jugendopern', *ZfMw* V (1923), pp. 506-45
'Die Bachpflege der Berliner Singakademie', *BJ 1928* (1929), pp. 138-71
Carl Friedrich Zelter (Berlin, 1932)
Die Singakademie zu Berlin, 1791-1941 (Regensburg, 1941)

Seaton, Douglass, 'A Composition Course with Carl Friedrich Zelter', *College Music Symposium* XXI/2 (1981), pp. 126-38

Serwer, Howard, 'Marpurg versus Kirnberger: Theories of Fugal Composition', *JMT* XIV (1970), pp. 209-36

Siebenkäs, Dieter, *Ludwig Berger, sein Leben und seine Werke unter besonderer Berücksichtigung seines Liedschaffens* (Berlin, 1963)

Sulzer, J. G., ed., *Allgemeine Theorie der schönen Künste* (Leipzig, 4th edn 1792; rep. Hildesheim, 1967-70)

Sumner, F., 'Haydn and Kirnberger: A Documentary Report', *JAMS* XXVIII (1975), pp. 530-39

Thomson, Ulf, *Voraussetzungen und Artungen der österreichischen Generalbaß-lehre zwischen Albrechtsberger und Sechter* (Tutzing, 1978)

Tiersot, Julien, 'Les oeuvres inédites de César Franck', *Rm* IV/2 (1922), pp. 97-138

Todd, R. L., 'The Instrumental Music of Felix Mendelssohn-Bartholdy: Selected Studies Based on Primary Sources' (Diss., Yale Univ., 1979)

'Of Sea Gulls and Counterpoint: the Early Versions of Mendelssohn's *Hebrides Overture*', *19CM* II (1979), pp. 197-213

'An Unfinished Symphony by Mendelssohn', *ML* LXI (1980), pp. 293-309

'A Sonata by Mendelssohn', *PQ* XXIX (1981), no. 112, pp. 30-41

'An Unfinished Piano Concerto by Mendelssohn', *MQ* LXVIII (1982), pp. 80-101

Türk, D. G., *Kurze Anweisung zum Generalbaßspielen* (Leipzig, 1791)

Turner, J. R., 'Nineteenth-Century Autograph Music Manuscripts in The Pierpont Morgan Library: A Check List (II)', *19CM* IV (1980), pp. 157-83

Weber, Carl Maria von, *Writings on Music,* ed. John Warrack, trans. Martin Cooper (Cambridge, 1981)

Weber, Gottfried, *Versuch einer geordneten Theorie der Tonsetzkunst*, 3 vols. (Mainz, 1817-21); trans. J. F. Warner as *Theory of Musical Composition*, 2 vols. (London, 1851)

Wehmer, Carl, ed., *Ein tief gegründet Herz: der Briefwechsel Felix Mendelssohn-Bartholdys mit Johann Gustav Droysen* (Heidelberg, 1959)

Werner, Eric, 'Mendelssohn', *MGG* IX (Kassel, 1961), cols. 59-98

Mendelssohn: A New Image of the Composer and his Age, trans. Dika Newlin (London, 1963)

Werner, Rudolf, *Felix Mendelssohn Bartholdy als Kirchenmusiker* (Frankfurt, 1930)

Wolff, Christoph, 'Bach's *Handexemplar* of the Goldberg Variations: A New Source', *JAMS* XXIX (1976), pp. 224-41

Wolff, H. C., 'Zur Erstausgabe von Mendelssohns Jugendsinfonien', *DJdM* XII (1967), pp. 96-115

Zelter, C. F., *Karl Fasch* (Berlin, 1801)

PART II

Inventory of Oxford, Bodleian MS Margaret Deneke Mendelssohn C. 43

Folio, description	Annotations, comments, concordances
[I. *Figured Bass and Fundamental Bass*]	
1r. Exercises *a* 3, *a* 4, C major	'd. 28sten' [August or September, 1819?]
1v. Exercises *a* 3, *a* 4, G major	'd. 23sten' [August or September, 1819?]
2r. Exercises *a* 3, *a* 4, D major, A major	'd. 24', 'd. 25sten' [August or September, 1819?]
2v. Exercises *a* 3, *a* 4, B major, D♭ major	'9 September', 'd. 19ten' [September, 1819]
3r. Exercises *a* 3, *a* 4, E♭ major, F major	'28sten' [September, 1819]
3v. Exercise *a* 4, C major; treble, soprano, alto, tenor, bass clefs	'Ende des Generalbaß Berlin d. 6 October 1819'
[II. *Unornamented Chorales*]	
4r. 'Choral 1', C major	
4v. 'Choral 2', A minor	
5r. 'Choral 3', G major	
5v. 'Choral 4', E minor	'B. 16 Obr 1819'
6r. 'Choral 5', D major	
6v. 'Choral 6', B minor	'war ganz ohne Gedanke verfertigt. 23 Obr 19. Z.'
7r. 'Choral 7', A major	'wird erinnert die Sache nicht für gar zu leicht zu halten. Z. 23 Obr 19'
7v. 'Choral 8', F♯ minor	
8r. 'Choral 9', F major	
8v. 'Choral 10', D minor, [Ach, was soll ich Sünder machen]	'B. 10 IXbr. [Nov.] 1819'
9r. 'Choral 11', B♭ major	'muß wenn der Baß fertig ist auf dem Fortep. probirt und verbessert werden ohne daß die Correctur bemerkt wird. Z.'
9v. 'Choral 12', G minor	
10r. 'Choral 13', G major, [Allein Gott in der Höh' sei Ehr]	
10v. 'Choral 14', A minor, [Allein zu dir, Herr Jesu Christ]	
11r. 'Choral 15', C major, [Alle Menschen müssen sterben]	
11v. 'Choral 16', A minor	'Die vordersten Choräle müssen alle noch ausgefüllt werden. Z. B. 13 Xbr. [Dec.] 19'
[III. *Ornamented Chorales, Migrating Cantus Firmi, and Gellert Chorales*]	
12r. 'Choral 17', F major	'Alle vorige Choräle müssen zurecht mit Tinte überzeichnet werden 20 Xbr. [Dec.] 19 Z'
12v. [Choral 18], B♭ major	
13r. [Choral 19], F major, [Freu' dich sehr, O meine Seele]	

Folio, description	Annotations, comments, concordances
13v. [Choral 20], F major, [Nun danket alle Gott]	'Die beiden letzten Choräle müssen noch schwarz ausgefüllt und reinlich abgerieben werden. Z. 3 Januar 20.'
14r. [Choral 21], C major	'Cantus firmus im Tenor. Erst wird ein anhaltlicher Baß, dann die eine Oberstimme und zuletzt der Alt gemacht, doch so daß alle Stimmen sich bequem bringen. Z.'
14v. [Choral 22], C major	'Cantus firmus im Alt.' '8 Januar 1820 Z.'
15r. [Choral 23], C major	'Cantus firmus im Baß.'
15v. [Choral 24a], G major, 'Gott, deine Güte reicht so weit'	Text by Gellert
16r. [Choral 24b], G major, 'Gott, deine Güte reicht so weit' [alternative setting]	
⌈ 16v. [Choral 25], G major, 'Dein Heil, ⌊ 17r. O Christ, nicht zu verscherzen'	Text by Gellert
⌈ 17r. [Choral 26], G minor, 'Was ists, daß ich mich quäle' ⌊ 17v.	Text by Gellert
⌈ 17v. [Choral 27], G minor, 'Was sorgst du ängstlich für dein Leben?' ⌊ 18r.	Text by Gellert
18v. [Choral 28], D minor, 'Erinnre dich mein Geist'	Text by Gellert
19r. [Choral 29a], G [?] 'Wer bin ich von Natur'	Text by Gellert
19v. [Choral 29b], D [?] 'Wer bin ich von Natur'	Text by Gellert
20r. [Choral 29c], C major, 'Wer bin ich von Natur'	Text by Gellert
20v. [Choral 29d], A minor, 'Wer bin ich von Natur'	Text by Gellert
21r. 'Pauvre Jeanette'	Text unidentified; voice, piano

[IV. *Invertible Counterpoint and Canon a 2*]

⌈ 21v. Exercises in invertible counterpoint *a* 2 ⌊ 22r.	'1. Nicht aus der Octave 2. Nicht 2 Quarten 3. Die None nicht anders als ob sie eine Sekunde wäre.'
⌈ 22r. Exercise *a* 2, B minor ⌊ 22v.	Concordances - PML; DSB (April–May, 1820)
22v. Sketches for canons *a* 2, F major, at the octave	See fol. 23v
⌈ 22v. Canon *a* 2, D major, at the octave ⌊ 23r.	
⌈ 23r. Exercise *a* 2, G major ⌊ 23v.	
23v. Canon *a* 2, F major, at the octave	See fol. 22v
⌈ 24r. 'Canone in 8va' *a* 2, C major 'minore nella 5ta' [at the fourth and fifth] *a* 2, C minor ⌊ 24v.	
25r. Canon *a* 2, C major, at the octave and unison	'12345678 '123456789 87654321' 987654321'

Folio, description	Annotations, comments, concordances
25v. 'Canone alla 2da' [at the second and seventh] *a* 2, C major	
⌐25v. 'Minore Canone alla 5ta' [at the fourth and fifth] *a* 2, C minor └26r.	
26r. Sketch *a* 2, C major	Ascending C major scale with countersubject
26v. 'Canone alla 5ta' [at the fifth and twelfth] *a* 2, C major	
⌐26v. '[Canone] alla 3ta' [at the third and tenth] *a* 2, C minor └27r.	
⌐27v. 'Fuga, Largo' *a* 3, D minor └28r.	Violin and piano; concordance - DSB (ca. May 12, 1820)
28v. 'Canon in der Verlängerung' [at the unison and octave] *a* 2, C major	'25 Mai 20'
⌐28v. Diminution canon at the unison and octave *a* 2, C minor └29r.	
29v. BLANK	
30r. BLANK	
30v. Augmentation canon at the unison and octave *a* 2, C major	
31r. Chorale, C major	

[V. *Fugue a 2 and a 3, Canon a 3, and Miscellaneous Compositions*]

⌐31v. Fugal exercises └32r.	'Thema, Dux, Führer, Soggetto'; see fol. 36r
32r. Sketch *a* 2, C major	See fol. 35r
32v. Sketch *a* 2, G major	See fols. 33v, 34v
⌐32v. Fugue *a* 2, C major └33r.	'Dux, Comes, Repercussio'; piano
33r. Fugal sketches *a* 2, D major, A major, F major	See fol. 34r; concordance - MDM B. 5, April 12, 1820
33v. Fugue *a* 2, C major	'Dux, Comes'; piano
33v. Fugal sketches *a* 2, G major	See fols. 32v, 34v
34r. Fugue *a* 2, F major	'Dux, Comes'; piano; see fol. 33r
⌐34v. Fugue *a* 2, G major └35r.	'Dux, Comes'; piano; see fols. 32v, 33v
⌐35r. Fugue *a* 2, C major └35v.	'Dux, Comes'; piano; see fol. 32r
⌐35v. Fugue *a* 2, G major └36r.	'Dux, Comes'; piano
⌐36r. Fugue *a* 2, C major └36v.	'Dux, Comes'; piano; see fol. 31v
⌐36v. Prelude and Fugue *a* 3, D minor, G minor └37r.	'Violino, pianoforte'; concordance - DSB (ca. July, 1820)
⌐37v. Theme and Variations, C major │38r. │38v. └39r.	Violin, piano

Folio, description	Annotations, comments, concordances
39v. Fugue *a* 2, D minor	'Dux, Comes'; piano
40r. 'In secula seculorum amen' Fugue *a* 2, C major	'Denn Dein ist das Reich / und die Kraft / und die Macht / von nun an bis in Ewigkeit. Amen.' 'In secula seculorum / Amen.'
40v. Andante, G minor	Violin, piano
41r. BLANK	
41v. Fugal sketches, G minor	
41v. Fugue *a* 3, G minor 42r.	Violin, piano; 'Cant. firm. Thema. Subjectiva'; concordance – DSB (ca. December, 1820)
42v. Movement, G minor 43r. 'Maggiore', G major	Violin, piano 'D. C. Il Min.'
43v. Movement, G major	Piano
43v. Canon at the octave 44r. *a* 2, G minor	Piano
44r. Movement, G major	Piano
44v. Canon at the octave *a* 2, G minor	Piano
44v. Prelude, D major 45r.	Violin, piano
44v. Fugal sketches, D major 45v. Fugal sketches, D major 46r. Fugue *a* 3, D major 46v.	Violin, piano; see fols. 47v-48r
46v. Fugue *a* 3, D minor 47r. 47v.	Violin, piano; see fols. 48v-49r; 49v-50r
47v. Fugue *a* 3, D major 48r.	Violin, piano; see fols. 45v-46v
48v. Fugue *a* 3, D minor 49r.	Violin, piano; see fols. 46v-47v; 49v-50r
49v. Fugue *a* 3, D minor 50r.	Violin, piano; see fols. 46v-47v; 48v-49r
50r. Fugal sketch, D minor 50v. Fugue *a* 3, D minor 51r.	Violin, piano; concordance – DSB, December 3, 1820
51v. 'Andante', D minor 52r. 52v.	Violin, piano
53r. Theme and Variations, D major 53v. 54r.	Piano
54v. Fugue *a* 3, D minor 55r. 55v.	Violin, piano
55v. Canon *a* 3 at the fifth, C major	Violin, piano
56r. Canon *a* 3 at the sixth, C major	Violin, piano
56r. Fugal study, C minor	See fols. 68v-70v
56v. Canon *a* 3 at the fourth and fifth, C major	Violin, piano
56v. Canon *a* 3 at the fourth and sixth, C major 57r.	Violin, piano

Folio, description	Annotations, comments, concordances
57r. Canon *a* 3 at the fourth and fifth, C major	Violin, piano
⌐57v. 'Allegro', C major │ 58r. └58v.	Violin, piano
⌐58v. Fugal sketch, C major │ 59r. Fugue *a* 3, C major │ 59v. └60r.	Violin, piano
60r. Fugal sketches, A minor	See fols. 62v-63v
⌐60v. Chorale, C major, │ 'Wer bin ich von Natur' └61r.	Text by Gellert; see fols. 19r-20v
⌐61r. Fugue *a* 3, D minor │ │ 61v. └62r.	Violin, piano; concordance – DSB, January 5, 1821
⌐62v. Fugal sketches, A minor │ 62v. Fugue *a* 3, A minor │ 63r. └63v.	Violin, piano; see. fol. 60r
⌐63v. Fugue *a* 3, C major │ 64r. └64v.	Violin, piano
⌐64v. Fugal sketch, C major │ 65r. Fugue *a* 3, C major │ 65v. └66r.	Violin, piano; 'd. 17ten Jan. 1820' [1821?]
⌐66r. Fugue *a* 3, C minor └66v.	Violin, piano
⌐66v. Fugue *a* 3, C major │ 67r. │ 67v. └68r.	Violin, piano; 'd. 20 Jan. 20' [1821?]
⌐68v. Fugue *a* 3, C minor │ └69r.	Violin, piano; 'd. 24sten Jan. 1820' [1821?]; see fols. 56r; 69v-70v
⌐69v. Fugue *a* 3, C minor │ │ 70r. └70v.	Violin, piano; 'd. 28sten' [January, 1821?]; 'Dux, Comes'; see fols. 56r; 68v-69r

Critical Commentary

This edition of the Margaret Deneke Mendelssohn MS C. 43 in the Bodleian Library, Oxford, attempts to reproduce Mendelssohn's exercises as faithfully as possible. The intent has been to transcribe the workbook with a minimum of editorial interference. A few minor revisions and additions, however, have been introduced for the sake of convenience. These include the addition of measure numbers, the substitution of treble or transposing treble clefs for soprano, alto, and tenor clefs, and the standardization of key signatures where Mendelssohn's usage is inconsistent. (Original clefs and key signatures are presented at the beginning of exercises where necessary.) Mendelssohn's treatment of accidentals, occasionally inconsistent, has also prompted some editorial suggestions: these are inserted, in brackets, either above the appropriate staff or before the affected note. The bracketing of systems, direction of stems and beaming of notes have been standardized. No attempt has been made, however, to correct faulty voice leading. A few specific cases are mentioned in the text above or in the commentary below.

A major editorial problem is encountered in exercises with several layers of corrections or revisions. Occasionally the original version cannot be established with certainty, due to Mendelssohn's thorough erasures, Zelter's covering of the original reading by an emendation, or the fading of the first reading, especially in passages recorded in light pencil. Any attempt to reconstruct lost or indecipherable material in an exercise is shown by the use of brackets.

Throughout the edition Zelter's handwriting is distinguished from Mendelssohn's by being in smaller type. Rejected readings are shown by diagonal strokes through note heads, rests and other symbols, as well as through entire bars: those in Mendelssohn's hand are angled thus \ ; those in Zelter's thus / . Mendelssohn's comments and marginalia appear in roman type, Zelter's in italic. In general it is not difficult to separate the two handwritings in the MS; Zelter's is usually thick and often coarse; Mendelssohn's tends to be much more refined and careful. Doubtful cases are mentioned below. Specific problems of transcription for certain portions of the MS, in particular the figured-bass and chorale exercises, are described in further detail below.

101

FOLS. 1R–3V: FIGURED-BASS EXERCISES (MEDIUM: BLACK INK)

Mendelssohn's realizations, uncorrected by Zelter, reveal several discrepancies with the figured bass. Often these may be attributed to the fact that each exercise was designed to produce a three-part and a four-part setting, even though only one series of figures was recorded by Mendelssohn. The numerals give the appearance of a casual conflation of the two settings. Thus, a figure intended for a four-part chord is not always appropriate for the three-part solution; vice versa, a signature recorded with the three-part realization in mind is incomplete for the four-part harmonization. For example, near the beginning of the first exercise (fol. 1r) Mendelssohn used the signature $\frac{7}{4}$, an appropriate choice for the three-part exercise, but inadequate for the four-part chord, which requires the signature $\frac{7}{4}\!_{2}$. Sometimes, however, the figures are not incomplete but incorrect. Thus, the fourth signature of the first exercise appears as $\frac{4}{9}$ instead of $\frac{7}{4}$ (or $\frac{9}{7}\!_{4}$ for the four-part setting). Mendelssohn frequently confused the intervals of the ninth and seventh, inverted the order of numerals (e.g. $\frac{6}{8}$ instead of $\frac{8}{6}$), and misaligned the figures of a particular progression (e.g. $\frac{6}{7}\frac{8}{9}$ instead of $\frac{7}{5}\frac{8}{6}$; cf. the end of the first exercise and the analogous, correct passage in the second exercise, fol. 1v). Mendelssohn occasionally omitted accidentals from the figuring (e.g. $\frac{7}{4}$ instead of $\frac{7}{4\sharp}$); a few editorial accidentals (in brackets) have been added for clarity, but there has been no general attempt to correct faulty numerals. Parallel fifths and octaves mentioned in the text are indicated by diagonal lines.

FOLS. 4R–11V: UNORNAMENTED CHORALES (MEDIA: SOPRANO, PRIMARILY INK;
ALTO, TENOR, AND BASS, PRIMARILY INK OVER PENCIL)

The chorale exercises form the most complicated portion of the MS from an editorial point of view. Chorales with a heavily corrected bass line are particularly difficult. In the edition the final version of the figured bass approved by Zelter is placed above the bass part, whether the figures actually appear above or below the bass in the MS. On the other hand, erased or canceled figures – those which are legible – are placed below the bass line in an attempt to preserve Mendelssohn's original solution. Ideally, then, a rejected figure (placed below the bass) should be matched with a cancellation or revision in the lower three voices. Thus, in Chorale 6, m. 11 (fol. 6v), Mendelssohn first harmonized the B of the melody with a seventh chord on C♯. His original figure, $\frac{7}{\sharp}$ (shown below the bass), in fact, is supported by the first version of the alto and tenor. Zelter, however, changed the bass from C♯ to D♯ and the realization from $\frac{7}{\sharp}$ to 6 (shown by the 6 above the bass, and supported by the emendations in the alto and tenor voices).

Such correspondence, however, is the exception, not the rule. Thus, in Chorale 1, m. 3 (fol. 4r), Mendelssohn first chose to employ a first-inversion seventh chord on the downbeat. His figure $\frac{6}{5}\!_{3}$ is accordingly placed below the bass line, even though no signs of this original harmonization survive in the inner voices. Zelter changed the bass and figure to accommodate a $\frac{6}{3}$ harmony, borne out by the alto and tenor parts. One must assume in this and similar cases that Mendelssohn's original signature was changed by Zelter before the chorale was completed, or that Mendelssohn's earlier solution was erased beyond recognition.

Fol. 5r: Zelter provided both the soprano and bass parts of this exercise.

Fol. 7v, m. 17: Zelter presumably neglected to change the first alto F♯ to E.

Fol. 8v: Mendelssohn notated the key signature for the soprano incorrectly; m. 5: the fifth of the chord is implied.

Fol. 9r: for a facsimile see M. Crum, ed., *Felix Mendelssohn Bartholdy* (Oxford, 1972), Pl. II; mm. 4, 9: Mendelssohn did not complete the bass and tenor parts.

Fol. 9v: much of the original version cannot be reconstructed (e.g., mm. 10ff.); mm. 17-18: Zelter's corrections to the alto and bass yield parallel 8ves which, curiously, remain unrevised.

Fols. 12r–20v: ornamented chorales, migrating cantus firmi, and Gellert chorales (media: primarily ink over pencil)

Mendelssohn's ornaments were first written down in pencil and then traced over in ink after Zelter had corrected the original note-against-note exercise. Usually Mendelssohn ornamented only one voice at a time. Occasionally, when he rejected an ornament, he turned his attention to a different voice, which he fitted with a fresh ornament. In the edition, the rejected ornaments, either canceled or erased in the MS, are presented with diagonal strokes to distinguish them from the other embellishments.

Fol. 14r, mm. 9-11: Mendelssohn mistakenly read the tenor cantus firmus in a soprano clef, which explains the inconsistent first version of the bass.

Fols. 15v-20v: Mendelssohn's punctuation of the texts, which sometimes diverges from Gellert's poetry, is observed in the edition. An exception, however, is Chorale 24b (fol. 16r), a revision of 'Gott, deine Güte reicht so weit', for which Mendelssohn omitted the text. Gellert's text is given here in brackets.

Fol. 15v: the first version of the soprano is on occasion difficult to decipher. A few questionable pitches have been placed in brackets.

Fol. 18v, m. 2: Mendelssohn doubtless intended the figure 4♯ for the second beat, not 6.

Fol. 19r, m. 8: this was left incomplete because Mendelssohn intended to omit it; m. 9 follows directly on m. 7.

Fol. 20v, m. 18: the first minim of the alto and tenor were at first mistakenly barred as part of m. 17.

Fol. 21r: 'Pauvre Jeanette' (medium: ink)

The text of this strophic French song, which serves as a kind of barrier between the chorales and contrapuntal studies, remains unidentified. Perhaps the song was sent to Mendelssohn's father, Abraham Mendelssohn Bartholdy, whose occupation as a banker took him to Paris during much of 1820. For a report of some musical gifts sent to him by Felix and Fanny, see Hensel, *The Mendelssohn Family* I, pp. 82-3.

With few exceptions the remainder of the MS poses no particular problems of transcription. Many of the exercises were recorded in ink, as if Mendelssohn were able to assert a new confidence once he had freed himself from the entanglements of the chorales. Zelter's corrections, written in pencil, ink, or crayon, accordingly appear far less frequently in the later stages of the MS. The following commentary is restricted to some special aspects of a few of the later exercises.

Fol. 24r, m. 7: Mendelssohn first attempted a cadence on a V^6 harmony, but then extended the canon by an additional measure, as the barring reveals; m. 11: the crosses are in Zelter's hand.

Fol. 27v: Slurs and staccato marks are in Zelter's hand.

Fol. 31r, m. 7: Mendelssohn evidently misread the tenor part in alto clef. He undoubtedly intended the pitches to be G♯–A rather than E♯–F.

Fols. 32v-33r: The first version of the C major fugue was written in pencil. Several corrections and revisions were also recorded in pencil. Much of the original version has faded beyond recovery. A second version of the fugue, written in ink, follows on fol. 33v.

Fol. 39r: Mendelssohn compressed the violin part for the concluding variation on to the treble staff of the piano part to fit the variation on to fol. 39r.

Fol. 40v, mm. 5-6: the slur is in Zelter's hand; m. 37 is canceled by Zelter.

Fols. 41v-42r, 50v-51r, 61r-62r: Mendelssohn recopied these three fugues as organ fugues in *MN*, Band II. They have been published in an edition by William A. Little as an advance release of *LAWFMB*, Series IV, Band 7 (Leipzig, 1977). These versions incorporate many of Zelter's revisions for the earlier versions in the workbook. There are a few minor changes as well. For example, for the G minor fugue, Mendelssohn compressed the end of the second entrance (fol. 41v, mm. 8-9) to one measure. For the first D minor fugue, on the other hand, he extended the pedal point near the end (fol. 51r, mm. 46-51). It is difficult to perceive why Mendelssohn recopied the fugues for organ, since the bass voice in all three compositions would seem to be too active to function well as a pedal part.

Fol. 42r, m. 24: the middle part lacks a fourth beat. In the version for organ in *MN*, Band II, Mendelssohn added two quavers, B♭ and A, for the fourth beat.

Fol. 44v: Mendelssohn incorrectly wrote ₵ instead of 3/4 for the time signature.

Fols. 46v-47r, mm. 1-10, 13, 14: the slurs are in Zelter's hand.

Fol. 53: Mendelssohn omitted repeat marks in mm. 8, 24, 40, 52, 60 and 68.

Fol. 60v, m. 13: Zelter revised the bass line but neglected to change the inner voices; m. 18: Zelter added the bar lines in soprano and bass.

Fol. 61v, mm. 17-18: Zelter added the tie.

Fols. 63v-64v: Semiquavers for the trills in the C major fugue are in Mendelssohn's hand, except for the trill added by Zelter in m. 51.

Fols. 65r-66r: Semiquavers for the trills in the C major fugue are in Mendelssohn's hand, except for the trill added by Zelter in m. 40.

[I. Figured Bass and Fundamental Bass]

105

9 September

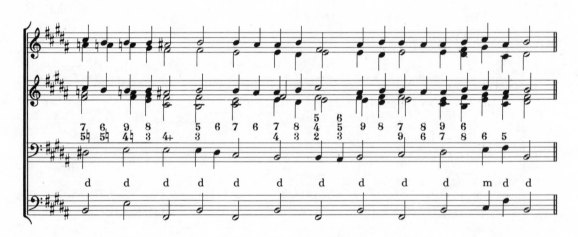

d. 19ten

d. 19ten

Fol. 3v

Ende des Generalbaß   Berlin d. 6 October 1819

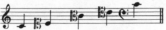

[II. Unornamented Chorales]

Choral 1
Fol. 4r

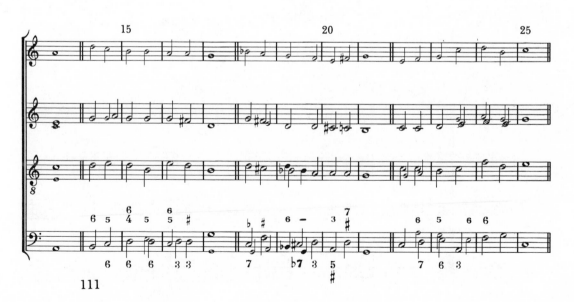

111

Choral 2
Fol. 4v

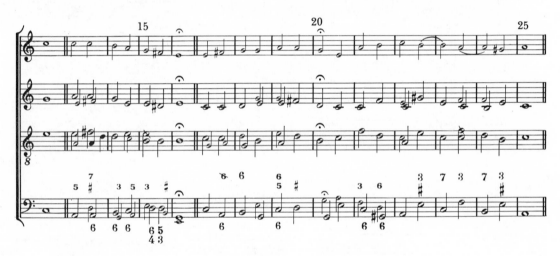

Choral 3
Fol. 5r

Choral 4
Fol. 5v

B. 16 Obr 1819

Choral 5
Fol. 6r

gis

Choral 6
Fol. 6v

war ganz ohne Gedanke verfertigt. 23 Obr 19. Z.

Choral 7
Fol. 7r

wird erinnert die Sache nicht für gar zu leicht zu halten. Z. 23 Obr 19.

Choral 8
Fol. 7v

Choral 9
Fol. 8r

Choral 10 [Ach, was soll ich Sünder machen]
Fol. 8v

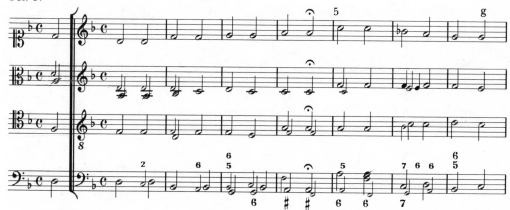

B. 10 IXbr. 1819

Choral 11
Fol. 9r

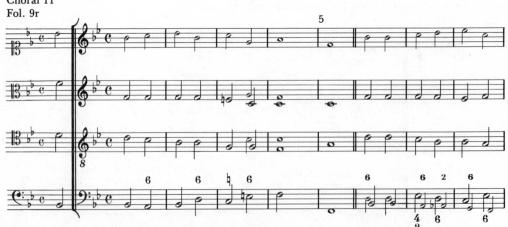

muß wenn der Baß fertig ist auf dem Fortep. probiert u. verbessert werden
ohne daß die Correctur bemerkt wird. Z.

Choral 12
Fol. 9v

Choral 13 [Allein Gott in der Höh' sei Ehr]
Fol. 10r

Choral 14 [Allein zu dir, Herr Jesu Christ]
Fol. 10v

Choral 15 [Alle Menschen müssen sterben]
Fol. 11r

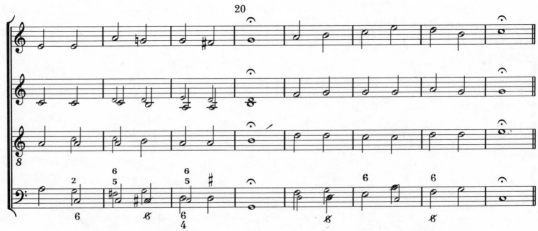

Choral 16
Fol. 11v

Die vordersten Choräle müssen alle noch
ausgefüllt werden. Z. B. 13 Xbr. 19

[III. Ornamented Chorales, Migrating Cantus Firmi, and Gellert Chorales]

Choral 17
Fol. 12r

*Alle vorige Choräle müssen zurecht mit Tinte
überzeichnet werden 20 Xbr. 19 Z*

[Choral 18]
Fol. 12v

[Choral 19] [Freu' dich sehr, O meine Seele]
Fol. 13r

[Choral 20] [Nun danket alle Gott]
Fol. 13v

Die beiden letzten Choräle müssen noch schwarz ausgefüllt und reinlich abgerieben werden. Z. 3 Januar 20.

Cantus firmus im Tenor.

Erst wird ein anhaltlicher Baß, dann die eine Oberstimme und zuletzt der Alt gemacht, doch so daß alle Stimmen sich bequem bringen. Z.

[Choral 21]
Fol. 14r

[Choral 22] *Cantus firmus im Alt.*
Fol. 14v

8 Januar 1820 Z.

[Choral 23] *Cantus firmus im Baß.*
Fol. 15r

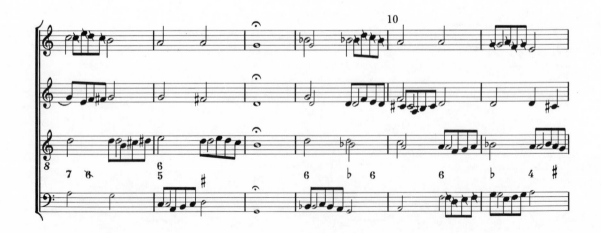

[Choral 24a]
Fol. 15v

Gott dei - ne Gü - te reicht so weit, so weit die
Du krönst uns

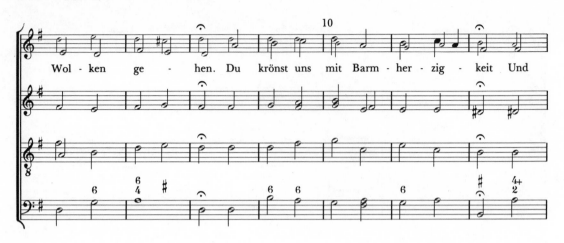

Wol - ken ge - hen. Du krönst uns mit Barm - her - zig - keit Und

eilst uns bei-zust ehen.— hen. Herr mei - ne Burg, mein Fels mein Hort Ver -

nimm mein Flehn merk auf mein Wort; denn ich will vor dir be - ten.

[Choral 24b]
Fol. 16r

[Gott, dei - ne Gü - te reicht so weit, So weit die Wol - ken ge - hen; Du krönst uns mit Barm - her - zig - keit, Und eilst uns bei - zu - ste - hen. Herr,

meine Burg, mein Fels, mein Hort, Ver - nimm mein Flehn, merk
auf mein Wort; Denn ich will vor dir be - ten!]

[Choral 25]
Fol. 16v

Dein Heil, O Christ, nicht zu ver - scher - zen, Sei

Dank mit De - muth oft und gern Und prü - fe dich in

Fol. 17r

sei - nem Lich - te, Und kla - ge dei - ne Noth dem Herrn.

[Choral 26]
Fol. 17r

Was ists daß ich mich quä - le Harr sei - ner

76

Fol. 17v

mei - ne See - le Harr und sei un - ver -

zagt Du weißt nicht was dir nüt - zet Gott weiß es

und Gott schüt - zet Er schüt - zet den der nach ihm fragt

[Choral 27]
Fol. 17v

Was sorgst du ängst - lich für dein Le

- ben? Es Gott ge - lass - en üb - er - ge - ben, Ist

Fol. 18r

wah - re Ruh und dei - ne Pflicht Du sollst es lie - ben

weis - lich nüt - zen Es dank - bar als ein Glück be -
- sit - zen Ver - lier - en als ver - lörst du's nicht

[Choral 28]
Fol. 18v

Er - inn - re dich mein Geist er - freut Des

ho - hen Tags der Herr - lich - keit Halt im Ge - dächt - niß

Je - sum Christ Der von dem Tod er - stan - den ist

[Choral 29a]
Fol. 19r

Wer bin ich von Na - tur, wenn ich mein Inn - res

prü - fe? O O wie viel Greul läßt mich mein Her - ze

sehn Es ist ver - derbt da - rum ver - birgt mirs sei - ne Tie - fe

Und wei - gert sich die Prü - fung aus - zu - stehn

[Choral 29b]
Fol. 19v

Wer bin ich von Na - tur wenn ich mein Inn - res

prü - fe O wie viel Greul läßt mich mein Her - ze

sehn Es ist ver - derbt da - rum ver - birgt mirs sei - ne Tie - fe

Und wei - gert sich die Prü - fung aus - zu - stehn

[Choral 29c]
Fol. 20r

Wer bin ich von Na - tur wenn ich mein Inn - res

prü - fe O wie viel Greul läßt mich mein Her - ze

sehn Es ist ver - derbt da - rum ver - birgt mirs sei - ne

Tie - fe Und wei - gert sich die Prü - fung aus - zu - stehn.

[Choral 29d]
Fol. 20v

Wer bin ich von Na - tur wenn ich mein Inn - res

prü - fe O wie viel Greul läßt mich mein Her - ze sehn Es

ist ver - derbt da - rum ver - birgt mirs sei - ne Tie - fe

Und wei - gert sich die Prü - fung aus - zu - stehn.

[IV. Invertible Counterpoint and Canon *a* 2]

Fol. 21v
No. 1

No. 2

No. 3

No. 4

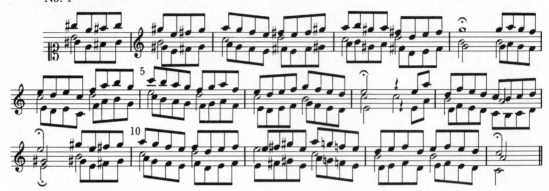

1. *Nicht aus der Octave*
2. *Nicht 2 Quarten*
3. *Die None nicht anders als ob sie eine Sekunde wäre*

Fol. 22r
No. 5

Fol. 23v

Fol. 24r
Canone in 8va

Fol. 24v

Fol. 25r

Canone alla 2da

Minore Canone alla 5ta

Fol. 26r

Fol. 26v
Canone alla 5ta

[Canone] alla 3ᵗᵃ

Fol. 27v
Fuga

Fol. 28v
Canon in der Verlängerung

25 Mai 20

Fol. 29r

Fol. 30v

Fol. 31r

[V. Fugue *a* 2 and *a* 3, Canon *a* 3, and Miscellaneous Compositions]

Fol. 31v
Thema, Dux, Führer, Soggetto

168

Fol. 32r

Fol. 32v

Fol. 33v

Comes

Dux

5

Dux

10   15

Fol. 34r

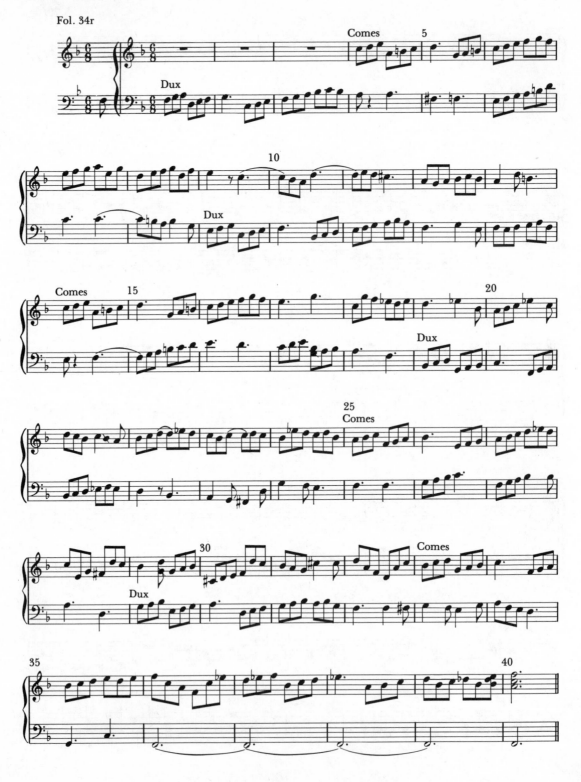

Fol. 34v

Fol. 36v

Fol. 37r

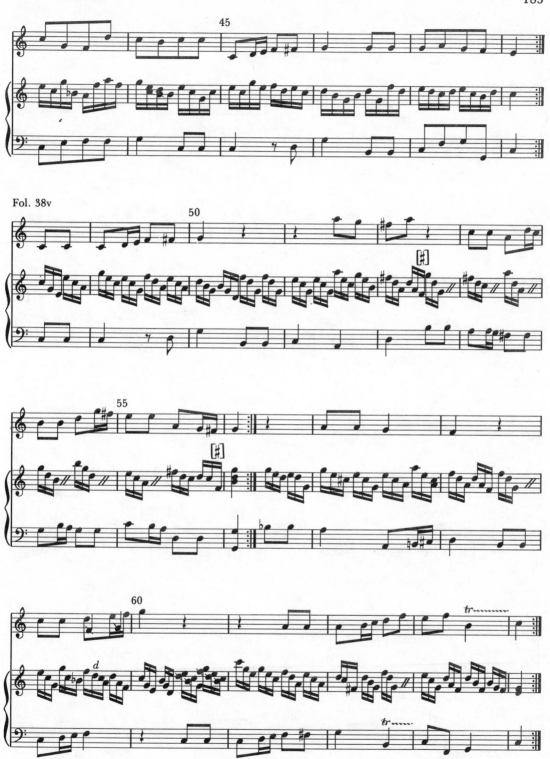

Fol. 39v

Denn Dein ist das Reich
und die Kraft
und die Macht
von nun an bis in Ewigkeit. Amen

In secula seculorum
Amen

Fol. 40r

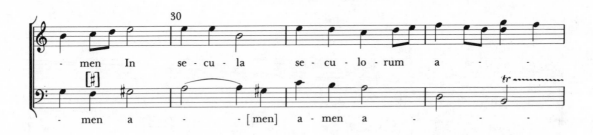

Fol. 41v

Fol. 42r

Fol. 42v

Fol. 43r
Maggiore Pizz.

C.A.

Fol. 44v

Fol. 45r

Fol. 46r

Fol. 46v

Fol. 47r

Fol. 48r

Fol. 48v

Fol. 49v

Fol. 50v

Fol. 52r

Fol. 52v

Fol. 53r

Fol. 54r

Fol. 54v

Fol. 55r

Fol. 55v

Fol. 56r

Fol. 56v

Fol. 57r

Fol. 57v

Allegro

Fol. 58r

Fol. 59r

Fol. 59v

Fol. 60v

Wer bin ich von Na - tur wenn ich mein Inn - res prü -

- fe O wie viel Greul läßt mich mein Her - ze sehn Es ist ver - derbt da - rum ver -

Fol. 61r

- birgt mirs sei - ne Tie - fe Und wei - gert sich die Prü - fung aus - zu - stehn

Fol. 61r

Fol. 61v

Fol. 62r

Fol. 62v

Fol. 65r
d. 17ten Jan. 1820 [1821?]

Fol. 65v

Fol. 66r

d. 20 Jan. 20 [1821?]

Fol. 67r

Fol. 68r

Index

258